MAHABHARAT
The Gateway to
POLITICAL MOKSHA

MAHABHARAT
The Gateway to
POLITICAL MOKSHA

Mukesh Bhardwaj

Vani Book Company
An imprint of Vani Prakashan Group

Vani Book Company
An imprint of Vani Prakashan Group
Head Office

4695, 21-A, Daryaganj, New Delhi 110 002, India
Phone +91 11 23273167 Fax : +91 11 23275710

Branches

Ashok Rajpath, Patna 800 004, Bihar
Coffee House Campus, Mahatma Gandhi Marg, Allahabad 211 001, Uttar Pradesh
Mahatma Gandhi International Hindi University, Wardha 442 001, Maharashtra
Goripur Taliya Para, 313, R.B.C. Road 24- Parganas (North) Kolkata 743 166, West Bengal

www.vaniprakashan.com
marketing@vaniprakashan.in
sales@vaniprakashan.in

Mahabharat : The Gateway to Political Moksha
by Mukesh Bhardwaj

ISBN : 978-93-5518-480-1
Journalism/Mythology

First Edition 2023

Price : ₹ 399

Printed at R. Tek Offset Printers, Delhi-110 032

Vani Prakashan's signature motif is created by Artist Maqbool Fida Husain

Dedicated to

Vivek Goenka

For preserving the letter and spirit of journalism despite severe challenges

Special Thanks

Ashwini Bhatnagar, Author and Thought Leader
Mrinal Vallari for Research
Arun Maheshwari and Aditi Maheshwari of Vani
My wife Jaya Bhardwaj, children Deeksha, Abhimanyu and Kartik

Introduction

The Mahabharat is a monumental script on human existence. The maha-kavya that runs into 100,000 shlokas (1.8 million words) boldly declares at the very onset: What is found here regarding the aims of human life – righteousness, wealth, pleasure, and release–may be found elsewhere. But what is not here, is found nowhere.

It is indeed a tall claim to make but even a superficial reading of the greatest-ever epic takes the reader to the highs and lows of human life that boggle the mind. The sweep of the ballad truly astounds mere mortals.

There have been many attempts to unravel the Mahabharat's historical growth and compositional layers. The oldest preserved parts of the text are from 400 BCE, though the origins of the story probably fall between the 8th and 9th centuries BCE. Scholars are of the view the final form of the text was perhaps arrived at in early Gupta period, 4th century CE. The original story, titled Bharat, was narrated in 24,000 verses which were later expanded to the 100,000-verse Mahabharat, the 'great tale of Bharat dynasty.'

We are all familiar with the main story of the epic–the story of Kaurav and Pandav brothers and their respective claim over the kingdom of Hastinapur. The dispute eventually leads to the horrific 18-day long war between them. Lord Krishna is central to this narrative, and is regarded as Lord Vishnu's avatar in the epic.

Strangely, Krishna's life early life in Mathura and Vrindavan is not mentioned in India's most ancient text. Scholar Irawati Karve in her book Yuganta: The End of an Epoch notes the omission and says Krishna makes his first appearance in the Mahabharat at Draupadi's swayamvara. He is referred to as a powerful Yadava Kshatriya from Dwarka. He and his clan had settled in the coastal city after being ousted from Mathura by Jarasandh, King of Magadh. Krishna's birth, childhood and teenage years are described in later Puranas, the Harivamsa and the Bhagvata but not in the Mahabharat.

She also says that early versions of the Mahabharat comprised only the first six chapters of Srimad Bhagvadagita. The last 12 chapters, including the famous 18th chapter, were added in later centuries. To substantiate her claim, Karve notes that the tone of the dialogues changes dramatically from the seventh chapter onwards. Initially, it is a man motivating a friend. It then changes to a guru with superhuman abilities preaching to a devotee, and, later, the guru reveals his virat roop --- the cosmic form of God himself. But Arjun and Krishna were intimate friends, Karve says, citing several episodes from the epic. Krishna did not even once try to become Arjun's messiah. The transformation in the Gita is therefore perplexing.

The gods of the Mahabharat though are classical Vedic. Kings and holy men perform many yajnas but temples are mentioned only four times in this humungous ballad. The mentions are inconsistent with the general scenario. They are probably later interpolations.

Another interesting aside is the Mahabharat does not mention whether the people of that era knew how to write. It tells us that all communication, even to distant kingdoms, were sent through emissaries who memorized the messages to be conveyed. There is no reference to the act of writing.

Small detail apart, there are a number of inconsistencies in the Mahabharat but they do not take away from the fact that it encompasses the entire spectrum of human dilemmas and emotions. There is no black and white here. No character stands out as an ideal. All of them have their duties, attachments, ambitions, foibles, grief, guilt and doubts. They are equally flawed and faced with existential misery. In the end, no one wins; everyone loses. The Mahabharat establishes the imperfection of human endeavor beyond the realm of doubt.

This is best seen in the Dharma vs Adharma argument floated by Lord Krishna. Though he is regarded as God himself, he is not spared questioning. He is doubted many times by Arjun, by the sage, Uttanka, and, most importantly, by Gandhari. She curses Krishna and his entire clan to perish. Other characters too are unconvinced by Krishna's advice and conduct. Duryodhan and Shakuni openly scoff at him as if he was human like them and not of celestial origins. Krishna's efforts are human too; they come with their own imperfections.

The Mahabharat is powerful because it describes men, their situations and their inadequacies in pitiless detail but leaves space for another critique, yet another re-evaluation of its colossal narrative. It offers its ideas on human existence and then negates them in one quick turn. The Mahabharat fascinates; in as much as it troubles us. Every episode leaves a disconcerting question. The doubt it creates however opens the window for another search.

When I saw the subject of the book and index on the main characters of the Mahabharat, I was immediately drawn to it. But at the same time I was surprised too that what new could possibly be said now? The first piece set my doubts at rest. Chapter after chapter, the book highlighted characters who reflected an attitude or an event. He explored through them, with considerable deftness, present-day issues of politics, identity, character, mortality, patriarchy, sexism, ambition, diplomacy, and much more.

His sense of timing in summoning characters from the Mahabharat for interrogation in each piece served as a useful and important primer on the existential crisis of the time. He placed them in their context and drew useful lessons for immediate future. And, like the Mahabharat itself, each of his articles was up for several interpretations.

Mukesh Bhardwaj's book is important because he clearly tells the contemporary story of people who are trapped in their insecurities, insufficiencies, manipulations, pride, ambition and vengefulness. Whether their cause is righteous is not important. What is critical is the end result. A community at war with itself leaves no winners.

—Ashwini Bhatnagar

Contents

Whenever, O Bharat, righteousness (dharma) declines
And unrighteousness is rampant,
I manifest myself.
I manifest myself from age to age to defend the pious,
Destroy the wicked, and strengthen dharma.

Lord Krishna in Srimad Bhagwat Gita

Surreal Political Mythology

On March 28, 2020, Union Ministry of Information and Broadcasting announced the re-telecast of its hit television serial Ramayan directed by renowned film-maker Ramanand Sagar. The repeat telecast of the religious serial was scheduled at a time when the Covid-19 pandemic had sapped the nation of its energy and people were uncertain about the future. The pandemic had created widespread insecurities, not only about the fate of individual lives but had also posed a serious threat to livelihood of a wide swath of people.

The Ministry said the repeat telecast of a serial, made in the mid-1980s, had become necessary in view of public demand for it. It would help them keep faith and mitigate the sense of helplessness and sorrow that Covid deaths and stringent lockdown had brought about. Ramayan was a motivating story of a divine, Sri Ram, and how he conquered adversity to emerge as Maryada Purushottam Sri Ram, the magnificent King of Ayodhya. Sri Ram's life and the establishment of an ideal government, the Ram Rajya, has never failed to instill devotion, hope and righteousness in people across the ages. The Ministry was perhaps convinced that the serial was the perfect anti-dote to the prevailing Covid-19 induced misery, especially after the Prime Minister had announced a prolonged lockdown on the country.

The then Union Minister of Information and Broadcasting, Prakash Javadekar, tweeted the date and time of the telecast of the serials–first the Ramayan, and, then Mahabharat, another hoary epic. The government was not expecting a prolonged lockdown. It was confident of controlling the virus soon. The serials served as a perfect diversion. The government also made it mandatory for all the cable operators to telecast the serials. To further underline the therapeutic effect of India's most loved epics, Javadekar tweeted his own picture watching Ramayan, along with the exhortation that people click similar pictures and post them on social media platforms.

The Minister's tweet however provoked a controversy. When the country was battling a deadly virus, the Minister was watching a serial, social media accounts mocked. The tweet had backfired. It soon disappeared from his twitter handle.

When Prime Minister Narendra Modi had announced the lockdown, he had pointedly harked back to Mahabharat too. Mahabharat was won in 18 days, we shall win the war on Covid-19 in 21 days, he had asserted with confidence. But Modi's battle-plans went awry from Day 1. His army was nowhere near the giants of Mahabharat warriors. The lockdowns were imposed repeatedly as the pandemic reigned supreme over a protracted period of time.

As India emerged among the top five worst-affected nations globally, the Health Department abandoned its daily press briefings to avoid facing uncomfortable and embarrassing questions from the media. Incidentally, the briefings were suspended because of another reason --- Home Minister Amit Shah and a number of other leaders, including chief ministers, union ministers, and MPs had gone down with the Coronavirus. The top official, who had been holding the press briefings, was infected, too. He had earlier pinpointed Tablighi Jamat for spreading the virus. It was indeed awkward to be in the same boat now. Moreover, the Health Ministry had been trying to present a positive picture of the Coronavirus even as cases cascaded in different parts of the country, especially Maharashtra, Punjab, Gujarat, Madhya Pradesh and Delhi.

The sudden announcement of lockdown in the country had created serious survival issues for the poor and the marginalized. Lakhs of migrant workers were forced out of their livelihood. With no real savings to back them up on a rainy day, they were reduced to starvation-like conditions. The need for survival triggered an exodus from all the major cities in the country. Thousands of daily wage workers started to walk hundreds of kilometres on foot to reach the safe harbor of their villages. The misery of a country undone by poor political and administrative foresight had now spilled into the open. Roads and highways were full of an endless crowd of men, women and children determinedly walking back to their rural homes. They were hungry and thirsty, penniless and distraught but the government did nothing. It sat on its haunches, and watched one religious serial after another. The poor, it was probably convinced, was paying for their past Karmas by undergoing the misery. The government surely could not interfere with what destiny had carved out for these hapless migrant laborers.

Modi, on his part, was smug in his beliefs. He believed he was a courageous big ticket decision- maker. No other Prime Minister in India, or even globally, has had the guts to challenge traditional well-informed wisdom. He had simple, quick-fix solutions to complex problems which he implemented with his trademark bravado. Black money and terror financing was fixed with demonetization, Hindu pride was taken care of by demonization of religious minorities, 'surgical strikes' on Pakistan were executed when the cloud cover had blanketed the enemy's radars, and, now Covid-19 was sought to be vanquished at the snap of his finger. On all these occasions, and many more, the decision-making resulted in countrywide chaos and unremitting wretchedness among the people. But, it did not matter. Modi's Chaos Theory had been well calculated to yield political dividends for himself.

It was therefore no revelation that non-migrants sympathized with the workers on the roads as they crossed their homes but quickly returned to their television sets to take in the divine emotions of Ram Vivah or the Draupadi Swayamvar. The devotion to spliced images of the divine on television screens was soul- cleansing for them after the sighting of human misery on the roads.

Karl Marx said religion is the opium of the masses. The response to Covid-19 nightmare needed this opium to soothe frayed nerves and the overall disquiet. Ramayan and Mahabharat fitted the bill. They gave the prevailing desolation in the country a deeper philosophical meaning. The epics wrapped the stark reality of the time in the gossamer of their fancy tales of palace intrigues, deceit, despair, defeat, and the final denouncement. The chaos passed.

The government had played a grand master stroke of 'epic' proportions. It was well applauded in circles concerned with power politics.

But this was just one part of the story. The other part was about the 'vultures.' The plight of the migrants was captured to a large extent by the mainstream media. International press too highlighted their tragic walk home. Public spirited individuals and organizations organized relief and aid for the returnees. No amount of help was big enough to provide succor to the thousands who were walking on sun-burnt roads with heavy loads on their heads and young children in tow.

The Supreme Court raised a query about the government initiative to alleviate the conditions of the hapless poor. The government responded by comparing NGOs helping the workers and journalists writing about the agonies of the exodus as vultures. Solicitor General Tushar Mehta, while defending the Central Government, recalled the story of South African journalist Kevin Carter, who had clicked a picture in Sudan in 1993. It showed a vulture waiting patiently as a child was dying of starvation. ``The picture was carried in the New York Times and got the Pulitzer Prize. But, after four months of the publication of the picture, the photographer committed suicide. He was neither a social worker nor was he running an NGO. But he had his conscience." The implication was obvious–Carter had a conscience while the NGOs and the media were the vulture without a conscience. They were 'prophets of doom' who only spread negativity, negativity and negativity.' It was 'an act of God' Finance Minister Nirmala Sitharaman had chirped in. And, by implication, God was the ultimate solace for the common man. The government relaunched Ramayan and Mahabharat to provide the necessary solace. It was a critical policy initiative of the Modi Sarkar to combat economic desolation and a health emergency in the country.

There are no migrant workers on the roads, the government lawyer told the court confidently. The media had conjured up the images and reports. "We are all honourable men here, we do not have to give assurances to each other as if we were lawyers," Mario

Puzo wrote in Godfather. But then, the Indian state was now heavily dependent on lawyers. It had no one else to state its case. They had all become victims of one master stroke after another unleashed by the Sarkar.

A Hindi film Bobby was released soon after Mrs. Indira Gandhi imposed Emergency in 1975. It was said in jest that the wildly popular film was an attempt by Mrs. Gandhi to divert the attention of the country's young from the problems of high prices and unemployment. Bobby was her attempt to immerse the youth in romance and other light pursuits so that they abandoned the agitational mood of the JP Movement. The melodious song 'hum tum ek kamre me band hon,' it was said, sought to give a happy veneer to an otherwise ugly situation. "The weather is pleasant. Go home and watch Bobby," she had famously advised.

Hence, it was not something unique to take the advantage of the screen to divert the attention of the people of the country from vital issues of public concern. The only difference was that the Sarkar chose religion as diversion. Though Shrimad Bhagwat Gita is a part of Mahabharat, but the actual story at no place conveys the message of selfless Karma. Even Arjun is exhorted towards his Karma with a specific target to install the Pandavs by dethroning Duryodhan. Krishna's pronouncements in fact do not tally with the overall story line of the Mahabharat. They rather mix religion with politics in an odd way to rationalize the war and the relevance of dharma in it.

Mahabharat was an effort to put the facts straight –like recorded history --- and, unlike Shrimad Bhagwat Gita, it had no moral or religious message for the mankind. It was a fascinating story of complex characters caught in their own circumstances and their effort to deal with the emerging situations. Had there been a lesson in the narration of events then, after Yudhishthir established the reign of Dharma under his command, there would not have been any of the similar troubles. Even Yudhishthir did not take any lesson in family values–he would not have headed to heaven alone. When given a choice to take one creature with him to swarglok, he chose his dog rather than any of the family members. In fact, the greatest war of the time was fought to knock down a rotten feudal system, but it ended with re-establishing the feudal system with a different lord.

In fact, Krishna held a mirror to the times to come. The world was yet in the memory of Ram Rajya. Krishna knew it was an utopia. There was no future in it. The world was becoming more complex. A new prism to look at the emerging realities was needed. Mahabharat was the new prism. It reflected the band of vices like cunning, cleverness, deceit, treachery, betrayal, enmity, revenge etc. through its single beam.

Mahabharat, in fact, was a bunch of stories that not only described the prevailing circumstances of its time but contextualized it in its own unique way. It presented the dilemmas and agonies of its characters in an amoral way. It spoke of various types of dharm --- raj dharm, mitr dharm, swadharm etc. --- in their own special context and space without an overarching imposition of what was right and what was wrong per se.

It established the relationship between the ruler and the ruled. Duryodhan was done away with after he had been identified as being dictatorial and unscrupulous. Simultaneously, Yudhishthir was established as the promoter and protector of loosely defined Dharma. Lord Krishna said that to topple the Adharma, Dharma had to adopt unrighteous methods but after the righteous reign was in place, equality and justice would prevail. But once the Pandavs come to power, the same old methods of so-called Adharm a come into play.

The Mahabharat may not be the better read book than the Ramayan but it had much more variety in its story telling than the Ramayan. The reader of Mahabharat soon finds himself caught in the rigmarole of story- within-a- story. The responsibility of learning the right lessons from it lay solely with the reader. Mahabharat offered no prescriptions on its own.

Shrimad Bhagwat Gita was the true spiritual achievement of Mahabharat. Had Lord Krishna not cascaded the source of this infinitive knowledge on mankind, there would not have been any war, and, if there was no war, there would not have been the larger message of the prevalence of righteousness. This war was nothing but an illusion created by Lord Krishna, it was Krishna against Krishna, his own army of Dwarka was fighting against him, and it was killed by his own side. The war was not between the Kauravs and Pandvas but between Me and I. It was the vain that everybody was fighting with.

Hence, there is no end to that war as it was fought to leave a message to minimize its occurrence. It was the same as the battle against the Coronavirus–there was no end, only containment. Lord Krishna knew that the sins of the life were not perishable and hence the purpose of the war was to create the fear of punishment of the misdeeds and vices of life. By this definition, the end of the Mahabharat was not the end but the beginning.

Property disputes are everywhere–from a slum to the posh areas. Brothers are yet killing brothers for the property and inheritance. And all this is happening in the name of Gita, and Karma. Everybody draws its own conclusion from the Mahabharat and the Gita.

Krishna said in the Gita that we should not be bothered about what others would say while doing our Karma. One should do them oblivious of the reaction. He told Arjun that he should overcome the thought of criticism in the post- war scenario. "If you would regress from doing your Karma then your image of a warrior would be destroyed. You will be ridiculed by the generations to come. You would be denied your exalted place in the next world for your cowardice. So, Mahabahu, wake up and do your Karma which is to fight the enemy at this moment," Ironically, Krishna added a reward to Karma which was against the very theory of selfless Karma propagated by Shrimad Bhagwat Gita.

The Gita justified violence for the protection of Dharma. Krishna left no doubt in his messages that violence was the only alternative to vanquish Adharma. The war led to fall of lakhs of warriors in the battlefield for no of fault of theirs, while it protected the pride of others–the kings, the leaders. Krishna himself killed his uncle Kans. He guided Bhim and Arjun to kill a number of others in the name of saving Dharma. However, the world has progressed far ahead of the theory of crime and violent punishment in all the cases.

In the new world however violence is no virtue even to preserve Dharma. Non-violence is the method. India gained freedom from the British colonialism not by the violent agitation but with Ahimsa (non-violence) shown by the father of nation, Mahatma Gandhi.

The Gita was actually an attempt to balance contradictory theories of violence and non-violence. India's current wave of nationalism has a Mahabharat ring to it. It has a selective interpretation of Himsa and Dharma.

Narratives of a civilization hold a mirror to the human values of the time. Indian civilization is soaked with human values and ideals of the time of Mahabharat but there are certain inherent complexities in them too. Abhimanyu's death is certainly an embarrassment for these values.

Abhimanyu : The Real Hero

Abhimanyu's blood soaked- body lay sprawled on the battlefield of Kurukshetra. Everyone was grief–stricken over the death of a boy-warrior who had made veterans run for their lives, first, by breaking into Guru Dronacharya's impregnable lotus formation, and, then by entering in combat against each of them singlehandedly. While ordinary soldiers wept over the tragic end of Abhimanyu's unrivalled valor, veterans strutted about, even danced and raised victory chants, to celebrate the macabre killing.

Abhimanyu had been persuaded to take on Guru Dronacharya's uniquely impregnable war formation – Chakravyuh– by his uncle Yudhishthir. The Guru had thrown the challenge of the formation to the Pandavs in the latter half of the great Mahabharaṭ war. Great warriors on the side of the Pandavs – Arjun, Bhim, and even the eldest among them, Dharmaraj Yudhishthir – had no clue how to penetrate through the complex and brutally taxing military formation and win the day for their army. Abhimanyu was the only person who could break into the axis but he did not know how to come out of it.

The story goes that while Abhimanyu was in the womb of his mother Subhadra, Lord Krishna had narrated the technique of breaking the Chakravyuh to her. Abhimanyu heard it in the womb. Half way through the narration, Subhadra had fallen asleep. The lesson had, therefore, remained half learned. But, Yudhishthir told him not to worry about it. "O lad, worry you not as we all will enter in your wake and provide you ample cover from the enemy onslaught," Yudhishthir had assured him.

Abhimanyu valiantly broke through the Chakravyuha the next day. However, Duryodhan's brother- in- law Jaidrath stood like a wall between the Chakravyuh and the Pandavs. He aborted their entry. Abhimanyu was trapped and killed mercilessly by his own uncles and other relatives.

While the Kauravs celebrated their victory, one among them, Yuyutsu, son of Dhritrashtar, castigated his brethren for this inhuman and cowardly act. "It is astonishing that you are taking pride in this killing, you should actually be ashamed of it. What you did is unworthy of warriors. You violated all norms of the battle and this death will go a long way to script your ruin. Be warned of your imminent death," Yuyutsu said with disgust.

Abhimanyu's death caused by a devious plan appalls the reader of the Mahabharat epic. The young man was simple and pure. He went in for a fair fight, displayed exemplary valor but was butchered in the most heinous way.

Abhimanyu was generation next for the Pandavs. In fact, generation next was very important for the Kuru race. A couple of generation back, King Shantanu had fallen in love with a fisher women Satyawati and wanted to marry her. She agreed to the proposal but with the condition that her child would succeed Shantanu as king. Shantanu was caught on the horns of a great dilemma. His son Bhishm was to succeed him and the line of succession was through him. The noble son resolved the issue for his father – he took an oath of celibacy. Assured of the rights of her future chidren, Satyavati married Shantanu. The marriage triggered a war of succession which finally culminated in Mahabharat which claimed the lives of millions of innocent citizens of the nation called Bharat.

Abhimanyu's story conveys the most significant lesson of the Mahabharat — the art of war can be learned in the womb of the mother but trickery and deceit required for victory have to be learned through experience. Abhimanyu was a young lad and he therefore became a hapless prey of the veterans. Arjun was incensed at his son's death. He vowed he would kill Jaidrath before sun down the next day.

Narratives of a civilization hold a mirror to the human values of the time. Indian civilization is soaked with human values and ideals of the time of Mahabharat but there are certain inherent complexities in them too. Abhimanyu's death is certainly an embarrassment for these values.

His character compels us to stop for a while to speak on the treatment meted out to him by his elders and the great men of the Dwapar age. All of them would have certainly blessed him with a long life had it not been for the war of succession. "Wait here. Pause and think. I am Abhimanyu. I am not a nobody of the Mahabharat. I am the generational representative of the time. I am the point of the history that would challenge even the teachings of Shrimad Bhagwat Gita. Go ask Krishna why is that my age was limited to boyhood? This story is a must for the prestige of divinity. This dialogue is all the more necessary because I am descendent of Moon God. O' Krishna, answer me if my father sent me for such a short time to earth because he could not tolerate my absence? I was born in the human race but what was my purpose? To be a victim of a slaughter at the hands of my own elders? What is my valuation? O' Krishna, you are my uncle. The almighty God. What did you do for me? Why did you allow this inhuman murder? Why was I made a victim in the war of succession? And most importantly, please tell me who is responsible for my gruesome murder?"

These questions though remained unanswered at that time and were left for their lateral interpretation. His small appearance got love from everybody but his sacrifice was neither discussed not properly elaborated, as war was at peak and there was no time. The battle was on and nobody had that much time for any such analysis.

Hence, his death remained obscured in heartless revenge first by the Kauravs and then by the Pandavs. In his life and death, he was a stimuli to aggravate the passion to intensify Mahabharat. This is the first death that raised an emotional and empathic surcharge in the battlefield. More or less the same kind of emotion and empathy is then seen in the death of Karan.

Abhimanyu raised one very significant question that is still relevant. Because till date feudal mindset justifies to kill son of one brother to empower son of another. Shantanu initiated this war of succession and his wife conceded to marry him only after he promised his yet to born son from her the successor to his throne.

The root cause of Mahabharat rests in succession. What would my son get? And why my son should not get all? In such a scenario why would we forget Duryodhan's son Lakshman too who dies alongside Abhimanyu at the same moment. Can we justify death of Lakshman? But this question would continue to haunt us till we allow feudal system to prevail.

Abhimanyu is the one character of Mahabharat who got everything exclusive. He is son of Arjun and Subhadra sister of Lord Krishna and Balram. Balram wanted his sister to marry Duryodhan but it did not suit Krishna's design of Mahabharat, as this would have changed the total script of the epic. Mahabharat is not a simple story of victory of good over evil, as was the case with Ramayan. Instead Mahabharat sets a benchmark that no evil should go unpunished and punishment was the only way to end the evil. Rather not only the direct perpetrators but those who stood neutral or witnessed the crime in silence also needed to be punished equally and mostly with their life. Or invincible warriors like Bhisham Pitamah and Dronacharya would have been spared as both were with the Pandavs in the heart of their hearts. But sparing them would have turned the tables on Pandavs in the battlefield.

Hence, no such alliance could have been permitted so Krishna provoked Arjun to abduct and marry Subhadra. Later he obstructed Duryodhan's proposal to marry daughter of Balram with Duryodhan's son Lakshman. This is pertinent to mention here that such partiality and bias leads to fatalistic enmity between the opposing parties. And this is what happened between Duryodhan and Arjun. Perhaps such fierce antagonism was necessary to give a motive to Mahabharat.

After Abhimanyu killed Lakshman, Duryodhan went mad with vengeance and taunted Dronacharya about his bias towards Pandavs. This was the simple principle of the feudal system, son for son. However, the war of succession led to loss of successors of both the sides. However, one Lakshman immediately goes in obscurity while Abhimanyu joins the list of martyrs and registered as the greatest warrior. His death needs to be avenged whereas Lakshman died like any other soldier. This is so because Lord Krishna is on the side of Pandavs. And since Krishna is on the side of Pandavs, they are on the path of Dharma.

Ironically, the role of Krishna in pacifying the battle never seemed sincere. A close scrutiny of events divulge that Krishna never allowed the possibilities to stop the battle be explored. He is not neutral. Despite his pledge to not wield the weapon in the war, he actually tried his hand when an enraged Bhisham chopped the heads of Pandavs' army like harvesting of the standing crops. Even otherwise he played active role to ensure victory for Pandavs by guiding Arjun at the crucial junctures. But he too did not come in the way of destiny and knowing well that Arjun was being taken away from the battlefield under a set plan of Dronacharya who promised to take Yudhishthir hostage if Arjun is misguided from the battlefield. Dronacharya had declared that it was not possible to capture Dharmaraj with Arjun present on the battlefield to protect Yudhishthir.

Krishna knew that it would lead to death of Abhimanyu but this was destined to happen and even the God decided to keep away from this. There was no rule to mention that was not shattered in the battlefield of Kurukshetra. Krishna wanted Arjun to kill everyone of the Kauravs' army and Abhimanyu's grisly murder was enough reason to ensure this. This one deceit was taken as a justification to all to come from Pandavs, from murdering Karan to killing Dronacharya. This battle took the toll on the children like Abhimanyu and Lakshman only to prove a point, to kill deceit with deceit.

The inhuman feticide of the future of Abhimanyu gives us a measure to test the history of feudal system. Great grandfathers, elders, teachers and warriors who were revered and worshipped by the generations showed their ugly face by breaking every sacred norm of the battle. The debris of hubris thus falls on the present and is never regarded as an ideal but remains something befitting for the waste basket.

Abhimanyu gives a clear message that the result of the battle would be decided by the narrator of the story. In case of Mahabharat, the narrator is Lord Krishna and since he was wholeheartedly on the side of Pandavs, their victory was already secured. Had the rules of war would have been honoured, the day would have ended in a better way for Abhimanyu and he would have gone back to his pregnant wife Uttara and distressed mother Subhadra by the sun set. But rules lost their sanctity in Mahabharat and hence a bright star eclipsed much before its time.

Gender is the sharpest weapon in any present-day discourse. The question of gender is not confined in the frame of male and female but has gone beyond it. Mahabharat laid the foundation of the third gender successfully when the greatest warrior was made helpless in front of an eunuch. Even when Arjun himself impersonates as Brihinalla, his heroism is wrapped in a softer form of humanity.

Arjun : Hero by Default?

Arjun is the accepted hero of Mahabharat. He was the best in the eyes of his teacher Dronacharya, who compromised his position as a teacher by denying to accept, first Karan, and then Eklavya, as his pupil on trivial considerations of caste because he knew that both had the potential to threaten Arjun's position as the best archer. Moreover, Drona was training Kauravs and Pandavs with a motive to exact his revenge on his friend turned foe Drupad, the king of Panchal.

Arjun was also Krishna's favorite. In the mid of the battlefield of Kurukshetra, when he looked at his elders standing against him, his belief is shaken, frailties of his character got the better of him; and, at a crucial time when forces from both the side were confronting each other in the battlefield, he put his weapons down and refused to fight.

Mahabharat is a struggle for establishing a societal set up that abides by Dharma. Arjun was tasked to protect Dharma. But instead of following the command to fight, he protested and sought justification of the impending conflict. Arjun, unlike the other ruthless combatants in the epic, is therefore a warrior with a heart. He fitted multiple roles too. He's a great warrior but doesn't mind acting as a eunuch. He not only learns music and dance but becomes an expert and trains Uttara, the daughter of King Virat, who gave Pandavs shelter during their period of incognito exile, in the arts. Arjun, therefore, is the accepted and projected real hero of Mahabharat. He displays the power of his authority, as well as skill and patience to emerge as the strongest character of the epic.

Ramayan and Lord Ram are most venerable in India. The holy book and Ram are worshipped by every section of society. `Hey Ram`, were the last two words that the Father of Nation Mahatma Gandhi uttered before falling to the bullets of Nathu Ram Godse. Ram-Ram is the most common form of greeting in the north India and the holy chant of the name of Lord Ram echoes both at the time of birth and death. It is most pronounced during funeral processions when the body is taken to the pyre amidst chants of Ram naam satya hai. Ram's name is the way to salvation

Mahabharat, on the other hand, failed to secure a sacred place like the Ramayan in India. Yet, it is the most important reference point in the cultural history of the country. Instructive tales from the epic illuminate lives of millions of Hindus. They form the moral compass on what is Dharma and what is a Adharma. Each character in the epic is clearly delineated along these lines with a backup story leading to its deed or a misdeed.

It is well accepted that history is nothing but a constant dialogue with the past. King Dhritrashtar was blind but he was given an option to have his eye sight by sage Ved Vyas so that he could witness the Mahabharat with his eyes. He refused. He instead requested the sage to grant the privilege to his aide Sanjay who would narrate the happenings at Kurukshetra to him as they took place. The first question he asked Sanjay was, "O Sanjay, would you please tell me who did first wield the weapon?"

At this point, the king was not worried about the outcome of the war but was concerned about how the future generations would remember him. He wanted to retain his honor in the future too. Sanjay, without fear of retribution from the old king, explained that history remember him as a king without patience and wisdom, and for his blatant nepotism.

When the discussion between Dhritrashtar and Sanjay was taking place, Lord Krishna was giving his updesh to Arjun which were compiled in the form of the greatest philosophical treatise in human history – the Srimad Bhagwat Gita

Every time period creates its hero and makes him immortal. Arjun is immortal and adores the walls of Indian households alongside Lord Krishna – the warrior with the divine charioteer ready to take on his enemies in the battlefield of Kurukshetra. Lord Krishna blessed Arjun to be the hero of the epic but interestingly, though the Gita is revered, the text of Mahabharat is never brought inside Indian households. It is believed that bringing a copy of the epic into the house would cause conflict among the inmates. Similarly, while stories of Draupadi, Duryodhan, Dushshasan, etc. are recounted and remembered regularly, none is named after them. Arjun, on the other hand, is loved as a symbol of courage and valor.

Unlike, Draupadi, Kunti and Karan, Arjun is not fully critiqued objectively because he was the chosen one. He falls beyond an objective analysis because Lord Krishna had endorsed him. He was God's own choice.

Arjun's heroism however is not without dispute. His acts of valor start with deceit and end with deceit. His skill as the greatest archer was challenged by Karan on the first day of its exhibition in the Hastinapur stadium. Had it not been for his shrewd teachers Kripacharya and Dronacharya, he would have faced a serious threat to his position. But the feudal system of monarchy could not afford a low caste to score over a prince, that too a favourite one, and hence was given a straw to hold to through the swirling tide of embarrassment in full public view.

Earlier, Dronacharya had similarly destroyed another potential threat by asking the thumb of Eklavya who was not even a student in his gurukul. Eklavya, who would have otherwise been awarded for his passion and determination to learn the art of combat, was punished because he would have snatched from Arjun the top position which his guru had reserved for him.

Trickery and cheating are the hallmarks of Mahabharat but people ignore them because of their reverence towards these characters. God was with them, they argue, and they were part of God's design. Sample this, it was ten days of the battle of Mahabharat and Pandavs realized that their victory was not possible unless Bhisham Pitahmah was on the battlefield. They were heads down thinking of a way out of this deadlocked scenario. Draupadi was livid that Pitamah had come between her enemies and their death.

But Pandavs had the advantage of having Lord Krishna on their side. He could provide solutions with his divine intervention.

He mooted a plan and Shikhandi was called next day to ride the chariot with Arjun. The greatest warrior of his time shot his arrows from behind an eunuch to turn the tables on the Kauravs. The deceit was proposed and approved by none other than Lord Krishna.

Take the case of the death of Karan, who everyone considered a greater warrior than Arjun. He had divine powers and was blessed by the Sun God with an impenetrable armor. Arjun killed Karan when the latter was weaponless and his chariot had skidded into a ditch. His charioteer King Shalya refused to help him with the wheel of the chariot that had sunk in the ground.

Prior to the assault, Indra had already taken the kavach kundal (divine shield) of Karan by disguising himself as a brahmin. And as if this was not enough, Lord Krishna exhorted Arjun to take advantage of the moment and kill Karan or face a possible defeat. "Don't forget that Karan was the one who called Panchali a prostitute and he too was among those who killed a weaponless Abhimanyu," Krishna reminded Arjun and this was enough to provoke Arjun to shoot deadly arrows at the world's greatest warrior.

Arjun also killed Jaidrath with deceit. After Jaidrath halted the four Pandavs' march behind Abhimanyu into the Chakarvyuh and Abhimanyu was ruthlessly killed by the Kauravs, an infuriated Arjun took a pledge that he would not allow Jaidrath to survive beyond sunset the next day. The Kauravs successfully hid Jaidrath till the sun had set, but here again Lord Kishna saved his hero from an imminent death by immolation. He had hidden the sun behind his discus, the Sudarshana Chakra. When darkness descended on the battlefield, Kauravs thought that the sun had set and as Jaidrath came out from his hideout mocking Arjun, Krishna recalled his Sudarshan Chakra. It was daylight again, and Arjun killed Jaidrath at this moment.

Arjun's bravery on the battlefield is actually by virtue of deceit that smacked of cowardice. He killed not only warriors like Bhisham Pitamah, Karan and Jaidrath and desecrated the principles of warfare but also Bhurishrava. He adopted the unfair practice of intervening in one-on- one combat. When Bhurishrava was about to plunge his sword into the debilitated Satyiki, Lord Krishna exhorted Arjun to intervene in the battle or lose his close relative Satyiki. Arjun completed the formality of protest and thereafter intervened in the combat. He shot his fatal shafts into the body of Bhurishrava. Interestingly, there was a long standing dispute between the clans of Bhurishrava and Satyiki. The former was also an enemy of Lord Krishna's clan. Bhurishrava was with the Kauravs. The unfair killing therefore makes it difficult to accept Arjun as a hero because of the serious transgression of the code of warfare.

Reading of history is always instructive because it describes a period of time and its people. It captures the ethos as well as the ethics of the period. Mahabharat took place thousands of years ago. For the first time perhaps in our cultural history, it recorded human conduct in shades of grey. It, in a way, closes the chapters on time periods when life was just black or white. The greyness of Mahabharat characters and war episodes are however sought to be justified through the presence of a divine entity on the side of the proponents of Dharma, the Pandavs.

The essence of Mahabharat is in the celestial song, the Srimad Bhagwat Gita, which deals with the question of ego, the lie in everybody. Arjun is obsessed with an exalted ego. The obedient pupil of his gurus put down his weapons and refused to do his duty. It is a paradox that the greatest warrior is actually a timid person. He is under the illusion that the war would be deferred if he refused to fight.

At this point, Lord Krishna made his grand appearance to teach him about the mortality and transience of the world. "It's only me that is immortal or your soul. Rest is perishable. Your soul is never dead, it lives on. A body is nothing but new clothes for the soul," Lord Krishna said. Gita is the philosophical definition of a person's existence and the inevitability of death. Lord Krishna conveyed Arjun his inferiority and thus rid of his ego. An enlightened Arjun then picked up his Gandeev (bow) to change the course of history.

Arjun has strong ties. He was Indra's son and Krishna's friend. He was not only a great warrior but a wise man too. What made him a hero was his patience and unmatched valor. A number of the male characters of Mahabharat are strong and powerful but they lacked the quality of wisdom and tenderness of heart. These qualities separated Arjun from all others, even from his brothers, especially Bheem. Even when he hid behind Shikhandi to fight Bhisham, he was conveying the message of gender sensitization.

Gender is the sharpest weapon in any present-day discourse. The question of gender is not confined in the frame of male and female but has gone beyond it. Mahabharat laid the foundation of the third gender successfully when the greatest warrior was made helpless in front of an eunuch. Even when Arjun himself impersonates as Brihinalla, his heroism is wrapped in a softer form of humanity.

Arjun maintained his poise when Draupadi was disrobed. It was Arjun who controlled Bheem after he lost his temper and was ready to attack Kauravs to avenge Draupadi's insult. These qualities of Arjun separated him from other characters and made him a hero. Despite the fact that Ashwatthama was among the horde that slaughtered Abhimanyu, Arjun spared his life because he was the son of his teacher, Dronacharya. For such moral values, Arjun was equally loved by his elders and the gods.

Mahabharat is a Dharmayudh, and at every step Arjun was on the side of Dharma. If he strayed from the path of Dharma, it was not his own doing; it was at the behest of either Lord Krishna or the circumstances. He was the only character who protested any drift from the path of Dharma. He raised objection to fight his elders before the beginning of the battle and refused to use Shikhandi as a bait and shield to compel Bhisham Pitamah to lay down his weapons. He later apologized to Bhisham when he lay on the bed of arrows for his act.

Arjun also refused to attack Karan when he was unarmed but Lord Krishna reminded him that Abhimanyu was also unarmed and alone when he was attacked by a number of warriors and Karan was one of them.

In fact, among all other characters, Arjun shone uniquely because he was the chosen one.

Mahabharat is considered to be grand celebration of life and death. In Mahabharat death means an achievement in the battlefield and is a synonym for life too. You die in the battlefield but live forever in the memory of the generations to come. Mahabharat is, in fact, the first ever narrative in our ancient history that discredits immortality. It explains that death is as equal a Karma as life is.

Ashwatthama : Curse of Immortality

Every hero and every villain dreams of immortality. They wish they live on forever, unaffected by time.

Even the gods wished to be immortal. The elixir of a deathless life was thrown up during the churning of the ocean – the Samudra Manthan. Gods and demons had, it is said, cooperated with each other to churn the ocean to secure many bounties from its depths. The elixir of immortality came out during the churning and the gods and demons fought to gain possession of it.

The gods devised a plan to deny the elixir to the demons. Lord Vishnu appeared as a beautiful woman Mohini and tricked the demons. Immortality thus became the privilege of the gods.

For humans and others, there was a continuous cycle of births and deaths. The freedom from this cycle could be achieved through good Karma in each birth. Lord Krishna said "The one who is born would die and even the creator of the world if he landed on earth with a purpose of leaving the most important message of Karma in a human life would have to die." Death or morality, therefore, is the natural closure for every birth till the time salvation or Moksha is achieved.

Mahabharat perhaps is the only narration that graphically depicts how immortality can be an unmitigated curse instead of being a boon through the character of Ashwatthama. The warrior had a gem embedded on his forehead that was granted to him as boon. It made him immortal.

Ashwatthama's unique distinction was never fully acknowledged as it had not been acquired by his personal effort of valor or austerity and penance. It was a gift and hence did not grant him a privileged position among his peers. Ironically, while everyone sought immortality, a characteristic reserved only for the gods, it was ignored in Ashwattama's case.

He was also Dronacharya's son who headed the royal gurukul for Kuru princes. He was allowed into the warfare school because of his father and not because he was from the royal family. Ashwatthama loved and regarded his father Dronacharya enormously but he angered him time and again over his friendship with Duryodhan. His father failed to persuade him to leave Duryodhan, who valued him as a friend like Karan.

In the royal gurukul, Pandavs looked at him as a student who had entered the gurukul because of his father. They mostly kept away from him. Duryodhanhowever made him his first friend in gurukul. Duryodhan gave him equal share in all the luxuries available to him in the gurukul. Ashwatthama was devoted to Duryodhan, though unfortunately, Duryodhan never treated him at par with his other friend, Karan.

Ashwatthama was also ethical. He vociferously protested when Dronacharya asked Eklavya to chop off his thumb and give it to him as guru dakshina. He accused his father of taking the thumb of Eklavya to make Arjun invincible. "This is unfair and does not behoove you. How can you do such injustice, father," he asked Dronacharya angrily as the great teacher remorselessly accepted Eklavya's thumb as fee.

Of Duryodhan's two invaluable friends, Ashwatthama was unique in his devotion to him. When Duryodhan went to Bhisham Pitamah to seek his blessings, the grandsire refused to bless him with victory. When Duryodhan expressed his displeasure over it, Bhisham said, "O Duryodhan, I cannot bless you with victory because I have already given blessings of victory to the Pandavs. But I can bless you that before you die you would have an expression of complete satisfaction on your face." The satisfaction was brought to Duryodhan by Ashwatthama when he gave him the news that he had `killed the five Pandavs.`

Karan could not match Ashwatthama in his friendship with Duryodhan. For Karan, his own identity as the most charitable person was more important to him than his friendship, or any other relationship. He, in a way, deceived Duryodhan when he donated his divine body armor despite his father, the Sun god's cautioning him about Indra. He gave away the armor to buttress his personal philanthropy.

Karan, in fact, considered his own image more important than victory in Mahabharat.

On the other hand, Ashwatthama asked a dying Duryodhan, "My dear friend, what can I do for you at this hour?" Duryodhan asked him to kill Pandavs if he wanted to see him die in peace. He then killed the five children of the Pandavs while they were asleep mistaking them for their parents. He informed Duryodhan that he had fulfilled his friend's last wish.

Ashwatthama came to know soon afterwards that he had instead killed the children of Pandavs. It enraged him and he shot the Brahmastra towards Uttra's womb to kill her fetus in order to completely destroy the lineage of the Pandavs.

Lord Krishna cursed Ashwatthama with leprosy. Till this day, it is said, the immortal warrior wanders through the world begging for an end to his miserable life

Mahabharat is considered to be grand celebration of life and death. In Mahabharat death means an achievement in the battlefield and is a synonym for life too. You die in the battlefield but live forever in the memory of the generations to come. Mahabharat is, in fact, the first ever narrative in our ancient history that discredits immortality. It explains that death is as equal a Karma as life is.

Mahabharat elaborately explains both types of death–physical and spiritual–in finer details. If we do not culminate after our time then we cannot achieve the stage of Moksha. By creating a unique character like Ashwatthama, who is forever between life and death, Ved Vyasa did something very rare; and, by keeping Ashwatthama alive, the great seer established the universality of Mahabharat. Ashwatthama changed with time and circumstances in the entire tale of Mahabharat. Unlike Duryodhan and Karan, who remained stable in the pursuit of their goal, Ashwatthama reacted to different scenarios in different ways.

He is shown to be humane from the beginning, but in the end when he saw his dying friend Duryodhan, he turned violent and raided the Pandavs camp in the night against all rules of the war and killed five sons of Draupadi. Rules of a fair fight had already been tossed away by the Pandavs themselves but Ashwatthama's act enraged Lord Krishna who punished him with a curse for his crime.

Ironically, Ashwatthama was not enraged when the Pandavs commander –in- chief Dhrishtdumyna killed his defenseless father when the latter lay down his arms after receiving the fake news of his son's death from the ever-truthful Yudhishthir. His deep angst over Duryodhan's defeat is a tribute to his devotion to his friend.

Lord Krishna established that death was the only justice that could be meted out to evil. Ashwatthama too decided to give the deadly justice to Pandavs after Bheem killed Duryodhan by deceit. He thought that it was fair to use Adharma to establish Dharma and attacked the Pandavs at night. He was however blissfully unaware that the principle was selectively applicable and he was not allowed to do his Adhrama.

The story of Ashwatthama tells us that even God cannot come in the way of destiny. Before the beginning of the war, Lord Krishna told Abhimanyu that after Mahabharat the world would remember him as the greatest warrior. Panchali listened to this and feared for the life of Abhimanyu. At this juncture, Lord Krishna told Draupadi that barring her five husbands all would perish in the war. But burning with revenge, Draupadi was ready to sacrifice everything to bring doom on the Kauravs and fulfill her vow to bathe her hair in Dushshasn's blood.

Krishna had vowed not to wield weapons himself during the Mahabharat war but he was twice compelled to do so; first, in the case of Bhisham when he activated his discus but recalled it. And the time second, he used it against Ashwatthama. It is said that the Sudarshan Chakra is still active against him though Ashwatthama has managed to dodge it because of the boon of immortality.

The entire Kuru clan perished in Mahabharat. Lord Krishna's own Yaduvansh suffered annihilation. But Ashwatthama is still alive. "You would run helter-skelter in search of death but death would abandon you," he was cursed by an angry Krishna.

In a fair game, Ashwatthama would have adored the crown of a hero for the gem encrusted on his forehead to make him immortal. But he was deprived of heroism because of his blind rage. His father Dronacharya did not consider him as a competent and deserving son and tried to give him everything on a platter. He and the Pandavs gifted him half of the Drupad kingdom so that he could live life like a king. Dronacharya loved him dearly but not more than Arjun. Though he trained his son to shoot the Brahamastra but did not teach him how to recall it. That's why he could not recall Brahamastra and it hit Uttra's womb and damaged her fetus. It was saved from total destruction by Lord Krishna who put his hand on Uttra's abdomen to blunt the impact of the Brahamastra.

Uttara gave birth to a child who was bent at eight places due to the impact of Brahamastra. However, this was only a temporary relief for the Pandavs as their race was destroyed later when snake god Takshak bit Uttra's son Parikshit to fulfill its vow. Perhaps, Lord Krishna intentionally let Prikshit be born so that Takshak'a vow was also fulfilled.

Ashwatthama was a great warrior but he failed to create an honorable place for himself in Mahabharat. He is the strongest character for his traits of friendship and devotion. His father's death by deceit changed his outlook towards the war and he himself killed his conscience and adopted deceptive and unfair ways to kill his enemies. It was the turning point of his character and he had an unceremonious and cursed exit from the scene.

Balram's voice was dismissed much like the worldwide trend of labelling any voice against the ruling dispensation or its supreme leader as seditious. It is punished through a number of modern day laws which can easily be called repressive. It is indeed an irony that modern day democracies promote the principle of 'love your government to love your country.'

The epic establishes the necessity of war [illegible]. Its message is loud and clear—a war is the ultimate and effective instrument [illegible] creator [illegible] Krishna [illegible] in the [illegible] war to ensure [illegible] is not weak[illegible] it may not be by itself cap[illegible] Dharma but there may be a few people who [illegible] full and final triumph.

Balram : The Unheard

Mahabharat is a saga of valiant songs of the heroes of the Dwapar age. It's a poem of valor and bravery of legends which have become an vital part of our folklore.

The epic establishes the necessity of war to eradicate evil. Its message is loud and clear–a war is the ultimate and effective instrument to establish peace. The creator of the world, Lord Krishna was himself in the middle of the war to ensure that Dharma is not weakened. Evil may not be by itself capable of destroying Dharma but there may be a few people who may impede Dharma full and final triumph.

In Mahabharat, almost everybody including Lord Krishna are for the war because that was the only viable option to annihilate Duryodhan and his evil caucus. Duryodhan too was more than eager to go to the war. With Duryodhan its crown prince, the palace of Hastinapur was reduced to a place of intrigue and conspiracy with Shakuni at the centre of the affairs. But there was one character that was a lone voice against the war–Balram.

Balram was Lord Krishna's elder brother. Through the epic, he called a spade a spade and when Yudhishthir lost the game of dice with the Kauravs, he held him responsible for putting himself and his entire family to risk. He entered into an argument with his brother Lord Krishna to say that Yudhishthir was not a child to accept the invitation to the game of dice, not once but twice, on the basis of some parochial royal norm of false decency.

He also made serious efforts to bring the dispute between the two sides to an end. The efforts however went in vain as majority of the stakeholders of Hastinapur wanted to establish their paramountcy through a war. The warring families did not want mediation.

Balram believed in peaceful coexistence of the Kauravs and Pandavs. He had enormous influence over Duryodhan who he had instructed in the art of mace fight. Balram was the undisputed top notch user of the mace though his own preferred weapon was a farmer's plough. He was therefore fondly called Haldhar, one who bears the plough, and was the leader of the agrarian rural class.

When the final battle between Duryodhan and Bheem took place, Balram was the referee in the one-on-one combat. Bheem cheated to incapacitate Duryodhan. At this, Balram said with regret, "I shall be proud to own Duryodhan my disciple and ashamed to accept that I taught you (Bheem) in first place." The utterance is no less important than the theory of Karma because it came from the person who formed his pair with Lord Krishna and is considered as an incarnation of Sheshnag.

He knew well that it was his brother Krishna who had passed the hint to Bheem to hit Duryodhan on his groin, the only weak part of his body. Balram was not oblivious to the fact that Duryodhan was prompted to cover his groin by Krishna when he was going to his mother Gandhari who wanted to turn him into steel by removing her eye band and transferring the power of her rigorous penance to his body. "Duryodhan," Krishna taunted him, "Would you go to your mother in a naked condition? Don't you have any shame left? You are a grown up man." Duryodhan then covered his groin with a cloth. It became his weak spot in combat.

Balram was not among the heroes of Mahabharat because he preferred to remain impartial. He did not choose his side and stick to it irrespective of its acts of omission and commission. He tried his best to ensure that the rules of the game are observed but when he was convinced that Lord Krishna had foreseen the events and also the ethics that were being employed to succeed at war, he slipped into the sidelines. He realized he could not avert the disaster by his own Karma, and, therefore, let destiny take over the two clans of Kauravs and Pandavs.

In other words, justification of Adhrama to establish Dharma and identification of heroes on this basis made Balram's values irrelevant in Mahabharat. He however remained as a shining example of non-partisan attitude.

His principle of impartiality helped to identify the talent on merit. It gave no room to favoritism or nepotism even as it raged unchecked all around him. Mahabhharat is full of episodes in which a select few promoted their own select few, ignoring all norms of fair play and justice.

There were no takers for Balram's value system and Mahabharat war became inevitable. It was said that the war had to take place to disseminate the larger message of victory of good over evil; of Dharma over Adharma.

Balram's voice was dismissed much like the worldwide trend of labelling any voice against the ruling dispensation or its supreme leader as seditious. It is punished through a number of modern day laws which can easily be called repressive. It is indeed an irony that modern day democracies promote the principle of `love your government to love your country.`

Let's put Balram in comparison with his compatriots to understand his character in a better way. Only two kings, Balram and Rukman, brother of Krishna's wife Rukmini, did not participate in the Mahabharat. Balram had taught both Duryodhan and Bheem. He did not favor any of the two and treated them equally. On the other side, we have Dronacharya who trained the Kuru princes but blatantly favored Arjun. Dronacharya destroyed Eklavya, and did his best to prevent Karan to learn the war-craft citing their low caste.

Balram, however, was not moved by such considerations. He appreciated Duryodhan's devotion to teaching imparted by him as well his flair with the mace. He loved Bheem too equally. Though it was clear to him that the future belonged to the Pandavs because of his brother's alliance with them, he did not alter his stance to be with the prospective unchallenged rulers of the country.

Later in the battlefield, the master strategist, the ever cunning Shakuni was shattered when mighty Kaurav warriors fell one by one to deceitful acts of the Pandavs. He worried about the fate of his nephew Duryodhan because Shakuni knew that Krishna had ensured that one part of Duryodhan's body remained highly vulnerable to a mortal strike. He was therefore not sure about his survival against Panadavs under the patronage of Krishna.

Duryodhan was Shakuni's main concern. He knew that after the great fall in the battlefield, it was only Balram who could get them justice and support against the deceitful ways of the Pandavs. He sent an SOS to Balram on the last day of Mahabharat.

Balram was well aware of the happenings in the battlefield. He was worried about his brother's role in the battle. He rushed to Shakuni but it was too late. Shakuni too had been slain in the great battle. Balram confronted Krishna and tried to make him see reason over his controversial role in the battle.

"Dharma established with Adharma would go against you in future, brother. History would record your role and you would come under the scanner for your favoritism and bias towards Pandavs. You are doing it the wrong way. In the incarnation of Sheshnag, I am though your acolyte but remember your partiality would ultimately go against you," he cautioned the Lord, adding that Lord Ram had punished Ravan for his deeds but had stayed within the limits of maryada.

Balram recalled the death of Bhisham, Karan and Jaidrath. "Every death is by deception. Who is actually fighting this battle actually, brother? It's not Kauravs versus Pandavs. It's Kauravs versus you. I implore you to shun your favoritism and let the last leg of the battle be joined and won on merit," Balram pleaded in vain. However, as a show of respect to his elder brother, Lord Krishna committed himself to adhere to the ethics of the battlefield in the last part of the war.

On his promise, Balram agreed to referee the one-on-one combat between Bheem and Duryodhan for the sake of a final outcome. Needless to say that due to his reputation of fairness, he was accepted by both the sides. In a mace battle, a hit below the belt was prohibited. Duryodhan was therefore not worried about his weak part of the groin. Duryodhan scored over Bheem in the beginning of the fight and consolidated it further with each hit. Bheem was on the back foot from the beginning and Pandavs feared first casualty in their most powerful brother who was said to be as strong as a hundred elephants.

Pandavs looked helplessly at their blood soaked brother who was now not even able to escape the blows of Duryodhan. And at this crucial juncture, Krishna forgot the word given to his brother and whispered into Arjun's ears, "Hey Parth, why don't you remind Bheem of his pledge to break Duryodhan's thighs where he invited Draupadi to sit in the hall of games?" Arjun looked at the lord in great astonishment and refused to do it. He said point blank that it was against the rules of combat to attack below the waist. Fearing the worst in case Bheem was not prompted, Krishna decided to take matters in his own hands. "Hit him, O' you great warrior. Why don't you fulfill your word Bheem?" He then patted his own thighs to clearly pass the vital hint.

Balram looked aghast at his brother but by the time he could register his annoyance and protest, Bheem had already landed fatal blows on the groin of Duryodhan. At this juncture, Balram disowned Bheem as his pupil and declared Duryodhan his valiant disciple. "I am proud of you," he told a dying Duryodhan.

Balram thereafter refused all invitations to celebrate the victory of Pandavs. He was the only one in Mahabharat to have many qualities of a hero but his peace- loving nature was of no use in the dynastic feudalism of the Dwapar age.

Balram boldly stood up to Krishna's favoritism towards Pandavs. He did not let the thrill and glory of war to move him and take sides. He was, in a manner of speaking, a Gandhian voice in the time of war. He preferred to attach himself with the soil and take the productive plough as his weapon and devoted himself to the betterment of the agrarian community.

Interestingly, the farming community that worships Balram still does not blindly toe the government line. The recent farmers' agitation against the Central government's three farm laws is a testimony to their resilience as well as their ability to protest unjust actions of those in power. The historic agitation was non-violent and was marked with the unique solidarity that characterizes the farming community. Their Karma lay in the simplicity and innocence of their actions, while their Dharma was to unflinchingly carry on with their work on the fields. The fine points of Dharma and Adharma which Krishna advocated are of no concern to them.

Balram was the unsung hero of Mahabharat. He was the humble son of the soil, playing by the rules even in the face of an unabashed display of pomp, power, arrogance and brute strength by the Kauravs, Pandavs and Lord Krishna. He wasn't a pacifist also. He carried his personal valor lightly. He was rather committed to common ambitions of common people rather than his own illusions of power and grandeur.

Mahabharat has several instances of heroism. For the first shloka to the last, there was constant confrontation between strength and wisdom. Sage Ved Vyasa created various heroes to depict traits of human value system but due to the demands of the story, they became too complicated that it is not easy to segregate them in order to identify the real heroes. Significantly, one lasting lesson of Mahabharat is that strength can only be useful if exercised with wisdom. It becomes a lethal weapon of arbitrary misuse otherwise. Strength can also convert itself into civilizational values if driven by intelligence.

Barbreek : **Unsung Hero**

Barbreek was the son of Ghatotkach and Mauvati and a grandson of Bheem. He was known for his bravery from early childhood. He was an ardent devotee of Lord Shiva who had gifted him three arrows as a boon. Out of three arrows, one marked all his enemies, another killed them, and, the third, had the capability of destroying the entire universe.

When Mahabharat battle was announced, every warrior worth his salt was keen to participate in it. It was the greatest ever war and men of action wished to join it to showcase their martial prowess. Barbreek too wanted to join it. He asked for his mother's permission. She blessed him but told him to help the losing side. "Dear son, every warrior is happy fighting with the winning side. But I strongly advise you to help the weaker party, as the powerful would be able to defend themselves. I can assure you that this way you would create your own special place in this war."

Barbreek took a vow to help the losing side and set out for Kurukshetra. Barbeek's vow caused concern to Lord Krishna. Kauravs would be the losing side and if Barbreek stood with them, it would turn the tables on the Pandavs. The war would never end, or it would remain inconclusive. But an inconclusive war was not what Krishna had bargained for. In fact, Lord Shiva's miraculous arrows were the biggest worry for him. They could ensure that the Kauravs were never fully defeated. Lord Krishna therefore decided to stop Barbreek from participating in the war.

Krishna intercepted Barbreek on his way to Kurukshetra. He impersonated as a Brahmin and said that he needed the head of a warrior for his veneration on the battlefield. He urged Barbreek to offer his head for the purpose. Barbreek agreed but asked Lord Krishna to empower him with special sight to watch the war even after his beheading. Krishna granted him his wish and established his head atop a hill so that he could watch the battle. Barbreek watched the entire war raising his valiant cries.

After the war ended, Pandavs wanted to know who was the hero of Mahabharat? Lord Krishna told them that this could only be decided by the head of Barbreek that had impartially watched the battle. Barbreek was prompt in his judgment. It was Lord Krishna was the real hero of Mahabharat as it was Krishna who gave direction to the war. "You are telling me what all happened in the war but I only saw the Sudarshan Chakra moving on the battlefield of Kurukshetra. O' warriors don't even think that this victory is your doing. It is Lord Krishna who deserves the credit of the war," he told the Panadavs and thanked Krishna for giving him the privilege to watch the great war and then judging it too.

Krishna blessed Barbreek. "O great warrior, you have performed the supreme sacrifice for this war. You would be remembered for your role and what you could not do in this war you would do for the time to come. You would always bless the defeated and give them the strength to fight. I bless that you would be worshipped on the planet till eternity".

Mahabharat is actually a multi starrer epic. A number of the characters can lay their claim to heroism but it is not easy to point just one person. Every character offers enough reasons to be adjudged its hero. Arjun was the one who was chosen to be the hero. He was privileged with certain favors, including divine powers and boons that made him stronger and dominant over others. He was Lord Krishna's chosen one too for the sermon of Gita.

There are those who were slotted as villains despite their heroic qualities. Karan was on the top of this lot. But he was cursed from the beginning to be insulted, cheated and defeated. His guru Parsuram cursed him that he would forget his teachings at the crucial juncture of his life. Duryodhan was a great warrior in his own right but he was the chosen villain of the epic. Eklavya, had he not become the victim of Dronacharya mechanizations, would have posed a serious challenge to the pre-decided hero of the epic, Arjun. All three–

Duryodhan, Karan and Eklavya–thus became anti- heroes. Another was Barbreek who was deprived of an opportunity to become either a hero or a villain. He was sacrificed even before he could pull his blessed arrows from his quiver.

Perched atop a hill to watch the battle, Barbreek had understood that it was not important to be brave or courageous. It was also not important that which side had more strength in terms of number of men, arms and other means of warfare. The most important thing in a war was the strategy and its practical implementation. The Pandavs were following the wake of Lord Krishna and had therefore become invincible.

He also realized the vacuity of the decision to stand by the losing side. Also, no boon could give a moral standing on taking sides. It can only equip you with strength to turn the tables but it cannot take you on the side of Dharma. Moral strength depended on the immortal aim to establish Dharma. But Dharma cannot win without a definitive strategy. They needed to be balanced in order to usher in the rule of Dharma.

A decision to stand by the defeated might give moral high ground but it would be an aimless achievement. Moral values are important only when they uphold social values alongside. Barbreek realized that to stand by the defeated without analyzing its position can hurt Dharma. If a defeated side was on the side of Adhrama then it did not deserve to be favored. Sometimes the losing side wraps itself in the deception of high moral values but it stands exposed the moment it is judged on the yardstick of Dharma. Kauravs were never on the side of the Dharma. They deserved to perish.

It was though on the contrary in Gandhi's India where non-violence was converted in to the most powerful weapon against the tyrant British regime. Gandhi valued non-violence but then everybody does not have Gandhi's intelligence to judge. People after Gandhi are using and misusing his teachings and his cardinal principle of non-violence to fulfil their vested interests. However, the history of India's independence would not be complete without the mention of Bhagat Singh, Sukhdev and Rajguru.

Barbreek clearly saw from his perch that if the winning side had the hand of God on its back then the name of God is brightly written on the forehead of the defeated side, too. Hence, claims of victory was nothing but a farce because even the win was transitory. Barbreek had, in fact, gained the power of truth and he would therefore straightforwardly decide on the hero of the epic. He realized that the battle was not fought to gain control of Hastinapur but to establish Dharma. He was hence free of the guilt of not fulfilling the vow to stand by the side of the defeated. He knew that a vow is not for self but for the welfare of the universe. It was a unique feat that the leading yeomen of Mahabharat –Bhisham Pitamah, Dronacharya and Karan–failed to achieve because of the narrow constraints of their own words.

Mahabharat has several instances of heroism. For the first shloka to the last, there was constant confrontation between strength and wisdom. Sage Ved Vyasa created various heroes to depict traits of human value system but due to the demands of the story, they became too complicated that it is not easy to segregate them in order to identify the real heroes. Significantly, one lasting lesson of Mahabharat is that strength can only be useful if exercised with wisdom. It becomes a lethal weapon of arbitrary misuse otherwise. Strength can also convert itself into civilizational values if driven by intelligence.

In Mahabharat, both the heroes to the villains were bound by their vows. The vows do nothing but roadblock the mobility of time and close doors on any possible and rational change in the putrid traditions of the time. Such takers of vows cannot be recognized as heroes. A vow taken for a purpose protects the false ego and leads to arrogance.

Barbreek was one such hero. He headed for the battlefield with a vow to be with the weaker side. It had the potential of altering the result of Mahabharat. Here again Lord Krishna came forward to stop him in his tracks. It was necessary that Barbreek stayed out of the battlefield for the predetermined result of the war, victory of Pandavs and annihilation for Kauravs, was to be achieved. Barbreek in fact was the unnoticed hero of the tale. He gave the basic mantra for the defeated, "Haare ko Hari nam."

Mahabharat tells us that human life is nothing but a gigantic puzzle. A number of saints, seers, writers, intellectuals and philosophers devoted their lives to solve it but in vain. The more you know about it, the more complicated it becomes. Nobody can claim to have completely decoded the intricacies of human life. Mahabharat attempts to elucidate several of such intricacies of human life and created characters that were true representatives of such complications. All issues are therefore sorted out by none other than Lord Krishna who had taken birth as a human being to guide people out of the labyrinthine of human behavior and show them their true purpose.

According to Mahabharat, there was solace in defeat, too. Death was true salvation from human life. Krishna called it Moksha. A human life reached its zenith when it opened the doors of Moksha by detaching itself from the love and affection of those whom it called its own. The success of human life was in unbounding it from the boundaries of various relationships. Needless to say that the sermons of Shrimad Bhagwat Gita were aimed at making Arjun realize the truth and emptiness of the human life. It could only be salvaged through selfless Karma.

Mahabharat established that mindless muscular power can only be a weapon for the wise. As such, history belongs to those who wield the weapon but not to those who become the weapon.

Bheem : Mindless Power

Physical strength or wisdom? Can physical strength be useful without wisdom? Bheem of the five Pandav brothers represented enormous muscular power. It was said that he alone had the collective power of a hundred elephants. He was credited to have killed a hundred Kaurav brothers, including Duryodhan and Dushshasan. He tore apart the chest of Dushshasan and drank his blood in the mid of the battlefield of Kurukshetra. He had vowed to drink blood of Dushshasan after the latter insulted Draupadi by trying to disrobe her in the hall of games of Hastinapur.

He killed Duryodhan, though deceitfully, by knocking down his thighs by the weapon of Duryodhan's own expertise, the mace. But, if Lord Krishna had not come to his rescue on the banks of the pond where the one- on-one fight took place, Bheem's bravado would have been punctured by Duryodhan.

History stands testimony to the fact that physical strength is always used, rather misused, by wisdom. Among Draupadi's five husbands, Bheem was the only one who would follow her blindly without giving a second thought to whatever she desired of him. Bheem remained at the beck and call of Draupadi whenever she demanded instant justice. Clearly, Draupadi believed in eye- for- an-eye type of justice.

The aim of Draupadi's life was to avenge her insult at the time of her cheerharan, disrobing. She lived to exact her revenge on almost every important person on the Kauravs' side. She cursed all those present in the hall of games after she was inflicted the humiliation. Only Vidur escaped the impact of her curse despite the fact that he too was present in the hall and only raised a meek protest, almost as a formality, to keep his hands clean of the stain. However, though Vidur was spared, Duryodhan's brother Vikaran was not despite the fact that he had vociferously protested her insult and exhorted his father Dhritrashtar to stop it. Panchali's curse inflicted a horrible death on him in the battlefield.

Draupadi and Bheem had their own court to try and punish people with death penalty, and despite the heartless killings done by Bheem at the behest of Draupadi, both of them found honorable places on the side of Dharma and Lord Krishna because it was so destined.

Bheem was armed with great powers and fought on the side of Dharma, but he has not been acknowledged as a hero in the fight between good and evil. The reason for the omission was that his strength was bereft of wisdom and there was nothing heroic in his deeds in the battlefield. Bheem personified brute power with his acts like drinking the blood of Dushshasan after tearing apart his chest or crushing Duryodhan's groin. He single handedly killed all of the hundred Kauravs yet he hardly won accolades for his role in Mahabharat. It was Arjun who became the hero, and Yudhishthir who became King.

Mahabharat is actually a story of various characters equipped with certain powers and qualities that were meant for exclusive purposes. These powers were divine, granted by the gods, which enabled them to meet any challenge. The powers were real for the believers and a sweep of the poet's imagination for others. But then, the entire philosophy of faith stands on the foundation of fantasy and fiction. Belief is vital.

In the design of Lord Krishna, Bheem was on the side of Dharma but he was armed with demonic powers and even had a demon son, Ghatotkach. It was fair for the Pandavs to use demons in the war to establish Dharma. Such a mixture of rakshakas and non rakshakas made the Mahabharat quite complicated. Had Lord Krishna not given his sermon to Arjun, the interpretation of characters of Mahabharat would have been entirely different. Every character on the side of Dharma had his or her own share of black and grey; of good and evil within them. Krishna however skillfully justified the shades for one side and exonerated them from any wrong doing, while holding the opposite party culpable of the same offences.

Bheem's character also provides the basis for understanding the man-woman relationship. What is more important–physical strength or wisdom? Did an ideal man need both for his woman, and, if yes, how much of each? Bheem lacked wisdom but he had enormous muscular power. He was, in a way, a killing machine, especially for Draupadi. Duryodhan, Dushshasan, Zarasandh, Hidimb, Keechak, etc. became his victims.

Draupadi liked Bheem. He needed no special justification to inflict violence. He had a simplistic approach and it helped Draupadi in extracting her revenge. She was, in fact, consumed with the revenge motive against the Kauravs. She lacked patience and commanded immediate punishment for the perpetrators. Her other four husbands were however not as rash and intemperate like Bheem. He was therefore her favorite.

Panchali would taunt Yudhishthir the most as he would try to calm her down in her moments of anger and anxiety. She first tried to use each of her husband to fulfill her wish to exact her revenge on different persons but they would try to make her see reason. Bheem was an easy prey.

During their incognito exile, Keechak, the commander of Matasya kingdom, first insulted her and then tried to molest Draupadi, who had assumed the identity of the Queen's maid. Enraged by her insult, Panchali first implored Yudhishthir to kill Keechak immediately but Yudhishthir did not agree and asked her to be patient and wait for the right moment as the killing might expose their true identities.

Draupadi took it as cowardice. She was not concerned that if their identity was exposed, they would have to undergo another round of exile for thirteen years. She called upon Bheem to wreck vengeance on Keechak. The killing of Keechak exposed their incognito status and had it not been for Bhisham and Vidur, Duryodhan would have sent them back to exile.

Bheem was a vicious mix of human and demonic force. Such a warrior is usually misused by others who know how to convince him to do their bidding. Draupadi never loosened her grip on Bheem. After the cheerharan, Draupadi had vowed that she would tie her hair when Dushshasan was killed and she had washed her loose hair in his blood. The four Pandavs remained quiet but Bheem vowed immediately that he would not only kill Dushshasan but also drink his blood. "I assure you, Panchali that I would tear him apart to fulfill your vow," he had declared.

The killing of Dushshasan made Bheem look like a demon. He let out a thunderous demonic laugh when he killed Dushshasan before he proceeded to drink his blood. Draupadi was satisfied with the act. Bheem had completely fulfilled her wish.

Bheem cannot join the row of heroes of Mahabharat despite his unmatched valor. His wanton slaughter of a hundred Kaurav brothers, including Vikaran and Yuyutsu, who had stood with the Panadavs on crucial turns, made him the face of horror. His detachment from wisdom never permitted him to understand the difference between good or bad. Both the Kaurav brothers were collateral damage for him. Bheem did not care about moral bindings. He did not spare them despite their ethical stand in favor of Kauravs enemy clan, the Pandavs.

In fact, there was nothing heroic about Bheem's character. A hero needs to be a good combination of valor and wisdom. Bheem had valor but little wisdom, he was neither a hero nor a villain. In fact, Bheem and Draupadi may have been labelled as villains had Lord Krishna not delivered the sermons of Shrimad Bhagwat Gita and justified the use of Adharma to protect Dharma.

Mahabharat established that mindless muscular power can only be a weapon for the wise. As such, history belongs to those who wield the weapon but not to those who become the weapon.

Mahabharat delved deep into the issue of identity, social as well as individual. The clan, family and extended family, were the social identity of the individual, who,
in turn, identified himself with his unique traits, whether gifted at birth or cultivated later in life. Lineage was of prime importance.

Bhisham : Man of Word

Bhisham, better known as Bhisham Pitamah, was the grandsire of Mahabharat. He was called Bhisham because of his Bhisham pratigya (word of honour). If he was the most important character of the epic, he was also the most indecisive. Like a number of other characters of the epic, he was also obsessed with his exalted ego that always came in his way. It delayed his response to the urgency of matters before him.

Bhisham was full of himself because he rightly believed that he could win any battle with his martial prowess. Pandavs could not win as long as he was on the battlefield. He was the biggest obstacle in Lord Krishna's effort to establish the rule of righteousness (Dharma) after demolishing unrighteousness (Adhrama).

He was also the only other person, apart from Arjun, to whom Lord Krishna delivered his sermons in the mid of the battlefield of Kurukshetra. Though was a difference between the two updeshas. Lord Krishna appeared in his angry incarnation before Bhisham and asked him to die honorably or suffer his wrath.

Lord Krishna appeared in his gigantic divine entity to Arjun in order to exhort him to pick up his weapons to punish all those who were on the path of Adharma, while Krishna told Bhisham to surrender and accept his death. "Pitamah, you have become the biggest obstacle in the way of Dharma. I may have to annihilate you if you fail to embrace death as per your own wish. All your life you have been by the side of Adharma, protecting the evil designs of Duryodhan, and even now during this decisive moment of the end of evil you are trying to hinder its way. Perish if you may by tomorrow, or I shall clear the path of Dharma with my own Chakra," an enraged Krishna told Bhisham.

Interestingly, Bhisham tried to be equidistant from both Dharma and Adharma. He, perhaps, thought that by remaining neutral he would save himself from taking sides. But after war became inevitable, he chose Kauravs as they were ruling Hastinapur to which Bhisham was devoted unconditionally.

The Kauravs were invincible till Bhisham was standing on their side as Duryodhan's commander- in- chief. He had also simultaneously declared he would not kill any of the Pandavs. Bhisham ruthlessly slaughtered a major part of the Pandavs army after Duryodhan provoked him with this taunts and jibes. "Pitamah, your body stands on our side but your heart remains with Pandavs. You are fighting for us but wishing victory to the Panavas. Why this hypocrisy? And what about your unconditional devotion to Hastinapur? If you are so inclined towards them, why don't you just leave the field and allow somebody else to take command?" an angry Duryodhan said on the intervening night of the eighth and ninth day.

Duryodhan's acidic tone and venomous words pierced Bhisham's heart. Infuriated, he promised Duryodhan that next day he would ravage the Pandavs' army and would then take Pandavs captive to end the battle. True to his words, on the ninth day, Bhisham cut through the Pandavs army and soon the battlefield of Kurukshetra was strewn with mangled dead bodies in a huge pool of blood. Bhisham's ruthless slaughter of the Pandavs' soldiers and warriors enraged Lord Krishna. What would the five Pandavs do if their entire army was routed completely?

For nine days, the battle was nowhere near a result. Bhisham Pitamah had countered every move of the Pandav warriors. This was not according to the plan of Lord Krishna to establish the rule of Dharma. Krishna had taken a vow not to wield a weapon in the war but the gruesome scenario of the battlefield inflamed him. He got down from Arjun's chariot and raised his finger to shoot his discus at Bhisham. But Arjun was quick to remind him of his vow and promised him that he would kill Pitamah next day because by then the sun had set and the day had come to an end in the battlefield.

Both Bhisham and Arjun considered themselves to be invincible but Krishna showed them their inferiority before the Almighty. The message was crystal clear, "You are nothing ... play your role so that destiny may take its course. Neither death nor life is in the hands of man. All you have to do is to perform your duty and make way for the next one to take charge." Bhisham then bent to the colossal presence of the Lord and requested him to let Amba, who was born as Shikandi to Drupad, to take credit of his death so that she also got her salvation.

Krishna then appeared to Bhisham in the full enormity of his personality and told him to surrender the next morning. After the beginning of the war, when Krishna enunciated the principles of Karma, it was before Bhisham's death that Krishna elaborated on his principle of Karma and man's transitory nature in the design of God.

Lord Krishna also revealed how Bhisham could be killed. "The grandsire would not attack a woman. Hey Arjun, tomorrow you would take along Shikhandi on your chariot. Better keep her on the fore and fire from her shoulder. Pitamah would immediately put his weapons down and that would be the only opportunity for you to kill him," Krishna told Arjun.

Ironically, Arjun, who on the first day of the war had taken the moral high ground of not attacking his elders agreed to the plan. Bhisham, the greatest warrior of the time, was thus incapacitated. Bhisham's life is a message for the generations to come that flexibility is any day a better option than obstinacy.

Bhisham had been with the boon of death by his own wish. As a result, even after Bhisham's entire body had been pierced with arrows Arjun had shot at him, he was alive in an incapacitated state. The warriors of both the sides watched in awful silence the fall of the invincible. Krishna was content that he removed the biggest obstacle from the path of Dharma. Arjun was embarrassed and full of remorse. The Kauravs were enraged over Pandavs' mean tactics to take down the warrior.

Bhisham's life is no less complex than a number of other characters of the Mahabharat. In the prime of his youth, he vowed not to marry to ensure the happiness of his father. The vow enveloped his entire personality in uncertainty. He believed that the

Pandavs were the rightful claimants to the throne of Hastinapur but found himself incapable of getting their right for them. He knew that Pandavs were on the side of the Dharma but he takes command of Kauravs' army to fight against them. It is a pity that the undisputed greatest warrior of the time had no badge of honor to wear in the great war.

Even earlier, he took on his guru Parsuram in combat but the battle remained inconclusive. His only claim to fame was his devotion to the house of Hastinapur and the abductions of various princesses for alliance with Kuru princes. It's a point worth a thought as to why he was hailed and acclaimed when he shied away from decisive action at vital points in time? He could have stamped his authority as a pitamah on the warring camps by being a fair arbitrator. He could not do so primarily because he was too much embroiled in his own rigmarole of vows and commitments. His vow made him a helpless captive to Hastinapur.

Bhisham also failed to take the moral high ground at the crucial juncture of the epic when Dushshasan disrobed Draupadi in full public view. He did not intervene as a family elder or even as a king. He cited his vow of loyalty to the kingdom of Hastinapur disregarding the duty to uphold its moral and social values. In fact, the pledge of loyalty had lost its meaning or relevance in the light of the atrocities that were being committed by the Pandavs on their brothers. Bhisham's non-committal stand on issues that were knocking the bottom out of Hastinapur's legitimacy was perplexing. He was aiding and abetting the destruction of the very citadel to which he was bound by a vow to protect.

Mahabharat delved deep into the issue of identity, social as well as individual. The clan, family and extended family, were the social identity of Blurb the individual, who, in turn, identified himself with his unique traits, whether gifted at birth or cultivated later in life. Lineage was of prime importance. Characters in the epic are therefore always identified with by invoking their parentage and clan name, along with their own name. Bhisham, the son of Ganga, took a stern vow to remain celibate so that children born out of the wedlock of his father Shanatnu and Satyavati ascend the throne rather than his own progeny.

The decision changed the course of succession in the Bharata lineage. It was a tough decision to make, and a momentous one too, because in an era that was obsessed with perpetuating dynasties and expanding numbers of the clan, Bhisham made the ultimate sacrifice of self. It triggered a tussle of succession between the sons of Pandu and Dhritrashtar that culminated in the horrific Mahabharat war.

Bhisham is the most complicated personality in the epic. It is not easy to analyze him. He had himself spurned the urge to perpetuate his own name and lineage and yet was fiercely committed to preserving it. He was celibate but went out of his way to ensure suitable brides for the Kauravs. His loyalty to the kingdom of Hastinapur was, in a way, almost maniacal. It defied common sense and simple logic. The fluidity of circumstances and changing times did not prompt him to review his decisions. He stood alone, undaunted and proud, on the burning deck refusing to either douse the flames or save himself from the inferno.

Bhisham was ethical in his own way. His ethics was however confined within his own narrow perspective of honor, dignity and statecraft. The view blinded him to the fact that he was not firmly on the side of Dharma. He was oblivious that he was championing the cause of Adharma while swearing in the name of Dharma. It did rankle several times, and, when it did, put him on the horns of dilemma and uncertainty. Strangely, he emerged from uncertainty not after having resolved it but deepening it further. Bhisham's inner conflict was as much convoluted as the war of Mahabharat was.

The consequences of Bhisham's decision floated from Satyawati to Amba and became the cause of his death at the hands of Shikhandi. Amba had been brought by Bhisham like a commodity and was married to Vichitravirya. The marriage caused immense guilt to Bhisham later on. He had abducted Amba for the pride of Hastinapur but he had failed to protect her according to the circumstances. In order to atone for his action of abducting her from her swayamvar, he offered to be killed by her.

Draupadi held him responsible for her humiliation too. Bhisham did not intervene when the Pandavs lost her in the game of dice and she was molested in front of this eyes by the Kauravs. Draupadi dared him, called upon him to act but Bhisham not only averted her eyes but also shut out her cries for help. The guilt rankled with Bhisham and when he lay on the bed of arrows in the battlefield he asked Draupadi for her forgiveness.

He caused misery to Gandhari too. He forced the unmatched marriage of Dhritrashtar with Gandhari. In return, Hastinapur received an in-house enemy, Shakuni, who vowed to destroy Hastinapur to avenge his sister's unseemly marriage.

Ironically, all these acts made Bhisham the shining star of Hastinapur. His mere presence gave Hastinapur an aura of royal invincibility. The brightest star on Hastinapur's sky began to lose lustre and fade into oblivion as the battle of Mahabharat began. It was indeed a tragic moment for the great Bhisham Pitamah when Lord Krishna told him in harsh words to lay down his weapons and accept a graceful death.

In sum, Bhisham could never distinguish between Dharma and Adharma. He stuck to his vows unmindful of their relevance in a fast changing world. He was, in a way, wholly concerned about the good in his selfhood rather than the larger good. He therefore virtually did nothing to dissuade Duryodhan from the path of Adharma. He was serving Hastinapur, he told himself and others several times during critical moments, and would be loyal to the decisions of its rulers – in case a Adharmic Duryodhan.

Bhisham's death was the critical turning point in Mahabharat. He is killed through deceit, and the unethical act got the validation of Dharma. It established for times to come that an immoral action was justified if it led to the restoration of Dharma. In other words, it was legitimate to use Adharma to vanquish Adharma.

Bhisham's life had an important message. It emphasized the collective over a single individual. It also underlined that Dharma is ever changing. It was free flowing in time and space like a perennial river. Bhisham was the rock in the middle of the river. The river flowed past him; he couldn't have interfered with it.

Bhisham stood firm with his vows. On the other hand, he vacillated on what constituted Dharma and how his action could be directed by it. He was hero because he was a moan of his word. Simultaneously, he was not a hero because he failed to exercise his discretion in favor of the larger good.

Deeply rooted in dynastic rule from the mythological times, India is a unique form of democracy that still flirts with feudalistic and dynastic systems. Twice in a year, when the tricolour is unfurled at the red Fort, we are reminded how difficult it is to sustain democracy in India. Every government, irrespective of its political affiliation, carries along dynastic leaders who own their political constituencies like private property. Tragically, no party has been able to either contain or do away with dynastic politics.

Dhritrashtar : The Blind King

Deeply rooted in dynastic rule from the mythological times, India is a unique form of democracy that still flirts with feudalistic and dynastic systems. Twice in a year, when the tricolour is unfurled at the red Fort, we are reminded how difficult it is to sustain democracy in India. Every government, irrespective of its political affiliation, carries along dynastic leaders who own their political constituencies like private property. Tragically, no party has been able to either contain or do away with dynastic politics. The Bhartiya Janata Party (BJP) that rode to a brute majority under the leadership of Narendra Modi, the most vocal baiter of the Gandhi family, too has not been able to rid the party of regional dynasts.

Leaders, who wrote the founding principles of equality in the country, blew these principles to smithereens to accommodate their wives, sons and daughters. The first Prime Minister of India Jawaharlal Nehru led by example. He passed on his mantle to his daughter Indira Gandhi. She in turn bequeathed it to her son Rajiv Gandhi, and so on.

It is indeed ironic that those who fought against colonial rule created their own political colony to capture power in the country. In the past, India fought against dynasties on numerous occasions, but every time one dynasty was replaced by another. The Mahabharat war is the classic example of one dynasty putting the country and its people at stake to replace another dynasty.

A democracy is known by the way power is gained. Power gained by deceit, cheating, false promises and blatant lies can only create a hegemony of selfish and corrupt politicians. We have in real terms never moved forward from the days of Mahabharat. India still accepts the concept of heirship and hence a majority of leading political leaders install their sons as their successors within their lifetime.

It was Dhritrashtar's love for his son Duryodhan that destroyed the entire Kuru race. Nepotism was indisputably the root cause of Mahabharat and it still thrives like poison ivy on India's democratic façade. Not only politicians but Bollywood celebrities, sports body office bearers and leading lights of several other spheres impose their wives, sons and daughters in positions of power. Dhritrashtar syndrome affects almost everyone in India. The difference between people is of degrees only; while some are blatant about it, others are subtle.

To have a better understanding of this happily accepted phenomenon of dynastic rule, let's travel back to the time of Mahabharat. After eighteen days of war, the Kuru race perished, barring a remnant in Duryodhan, who was hiding in a pond fearing death at the hands of Bheem. Gandhari had already cursed Krishna's Yadu vansh of destruction. Triumphant Pandavs were hardly the proud winners as they surveyed the blood sodden battleground of Kurukshetra littered with lakhs of dead bodies, including those of the greatest warriors of their time. The skyline was dominated by vultures and the ground was raided by moths, dogs and swine feasting on the corpses. Hope lay buried under the heap of bodies.

Hastinapur was ruined but the King was yet alive. He was luckily blind, and hence unable to have first-hand experience of death and destruction around him. But he knew the facts. They had been narrated to him by Sanjay in vivid detail. But they did not have the same impact on him in the absence of his own sight.

Despite the bloodshed, Dhritrashtar still sought vengeance. He sought a meeting with the victorious Pandavs because he wanted to strangle Bheem during an embrace. He wanted Bheem dead because he had killed Dushasan and his favorite son Duryodhan.

Lord Krishna had anticipated Dhritrashtar's thirst for revenge. He put a stone statue of Bheem before the King of Hastinapur in replace of Bheem himself. Dhritrashtar possessed great physical power. He had gained it through hard penance. He embraced the statue and crushed it to pieces. Dhritrashtar wept bitterly when he realized he had been tricked and his motive had been exposed. Dhritrashtar was indeed blind in more ways than one. He was blind to the reality before him, as he was blind to the outcomes of his actions.

Dhritrashtar's disability affected him severely. Though he had all princely qualities, lack of sight frustrated him to no end. He clung to his family as his entire support system ignoring the larger issues of ethics and public interest. On a number of occasions, Dhritrashtar was on the horns of a dilemma. He tried to weight the pros and cons of his decisions – even leaning towards doing what was right --- but, on each occasion his love of Duryodhan swung him away from the path of Dharma. Interestingly, though Dhritrashtar tried to kill Bheem to extract his revenge, he was affectionate towards the other Pandavs during the same meeting. He asked for their forgiveness. At that moment too, he was as helpless as he was when Duryodhan had first denied the claim of the Pandavs. In fact, at every step during the Mahabharat saga, Dhritrashtar turned a 'blind' eye to everything except the self-serving interest of his immediate family.

Dhritrashtar's love for his son was not only a feudal wish but a patriarchal one, too. Feudalism and patriarchy are closely intertwined and supplement each other. Under this system, the king has a self-proclaimed right over everything, and, through the principle of inheritance, the son is his rightful heir.

In modern India, democracy did not come after a struggle against autocracy of ancient kingdoms. It was achieved against British colonialism. A number of feudal lords and regional royals also rose against the British with their demand for an independent India. They became our national heroes. There was no dearth of princely states too which stood by the side of the British hoping they would survive independently after the British surrendered their rule over the country.

In 1947, when India won its independence, it was faced with more than 562 independent states. Lord Mountbatten gave these states the option of either remaining independent, or merging with newly created nations of Pakistan and India. Then Prime Jawaharlal Nehru and Home Minister Sardar Vallabh Bhai Patel understood that if these small states were allowed to carry on as sovereign entities, they would create problems for the country and may become an instrument in the hands of colonial powers. Patel took two years to bring the states to terms with the Indian state. It was to the credit of Patel that states like Kashmir, Junagarh and Hyderabad that had tried to assert their sovereignty were firmly amalgamated into the Indian Union. The remaining part of the complex merger was finished by former Prime Minister Indira Gandhi who stopped the provision of privy purses for the successors of the princely states. The act finally threw the last remnants of the feudal system into the waste paper basket.

Post- independence, Indian democratic values developed as a positive consequence of the colonial rule. Several national leaders imbibed the spirit and letter of modern democratic governance from their exposure to ideas that were thriving in the West. The seeds of dynastic rule and feudalism went dormant for a while.

They however soon emerged as politics took a firm hold on the Indian democratic system. The rajas and maharajas of pre-independent India who had adopted the role of people's representatives in Parliament and elsewhere made a comeback. They insisted on recalling the old system of feudal lordship. It started a new political breed of non-royal --- the average neta in the vicinity --- perpetuating the democratic privilege on his progeny. Political destinies therefore took hold of the entire political system.

Congress has been truly nurturing the system of inheritance though it was soundly defeated, first in 2014, and then in 2019. Prime Minister Narendra Modi won because he capitalized on the dynastic politics of the Congress, derisively calling Rahul Gandhi as Yuvraj thereby underlining the divine right to rule of the Nehru-Gandhi clan. The Congress had no answer to this charge. Rahul Gandhi rather lent credence to it during a speech in Berkley when he tried to justify the system of succession by saying that India was a nation where a son of a king is considered his natural successor.

Speaking at the Institute of International Studies at University of California, Berkeley, he said, "Most of the country runs like this. So, don't go after me." Dynastic politics was common to all parties in India, he said. The Hindustan Times (September 12, 2017) noted in its report that "Gandhi is the fifth generation of the Nehru-Gandhi family in politics. His father Rajiv Gandhi, grand-mother Indira Gandhi and great-grandfather (Jawaharlal Nehru) all served as prime ministers."

He said: "Akhilesh Yadav is a dynast, Mr Stalin (DMK supremo M Karunanidhi's son) is a dynast, Mr (Prem Kumar) Dhumal's son (Anurag Thakur of the BJP) is a dynast. Even Mr Abhishek Bachchan is a dynast, also Mr Ambani...That's what happens in India and just the way India runs. The real question is if that person is a capable, sensitive person."

The statement gave the ruling BJP enough ammunition to go after him lock stock and barrel. It called Radhul Gandhi a "failed dynast". It helped in BJP riding back to power in 2019 with even a bigger mandate.

But, the fact is that Rahul Gandhi wasn't wrong. He had put across a fact of contemporary Indian politics in a straight forward manner. After independence, all the political alternatives to Congress– the nationalists, socialists and Lohiaites --- soon turned into political dynasties with leaders handing over their political inheritance to their competent/incompetent sons like personal property. They were all faint shadows of Dhritrashtar, and, tragically, took a heavy toll on contemporary Indian political ethos. Even Lord Krishna too might have been peeved at the rot Dhristrashtar's unsavory legacy had descended into. The modern Dhritrashtars don't accept anybody other than their own families even if it means destroying the political parties and ideologies they represent.

The BJP made dynastic rule a big issue in the 2014 election and then again in 2019. It lambasted the Congress for perpetuating family rule over rule of the most deserving. But no sooner it came to power, it too fell deep into the sludge. A number of its leaders allocated political constituencies to their wards. The hypocrisy of their act was compounded by the unrelenting tirade against the Congress over nepotism while nourishing it in the organizations.

The Congress lost several elections, including two back-to-back Lok Sabha elections, because the charge of 'family rule' stuck to it like wet mud on freshly washed clothes. It needed a change, but it refused to even acknowledge the need for it. It carried on solemnly, preferring to lose elections and popular appeal rather take corrective action. In a manner of speaking, it turned a blind eye to the writing on the wall. It perhaps reasoned that the issue was unimportant because it was only a matter of time before the Modi-led BJP crushed itself under the weight of its rash, irrational and selective policies. Strangely, it wanted the BJP to fail in order to vindicate the failure of its own dynastic politics.

Dhritrashtar and his blindness to the need of the hour perhaps symbolizes whatever is wrong in contemporary legacy politics. Though the Congress pioneered it to a large extent, it was the BJP and regional political satraps who cemented it firmly in the routine of democratic life. They normalized the exceptional practice of son succeeding the father in public life. 'Political royalty' and its divine right to acquire the people's mandate by hook or crook have been sanctified in a system that claims to be democratic but is aristocratic through its length and breath. Only a few, because of their lineage, have the 'pass' to sit at the high table of power and pelf. The ordinary political worker has become a daily wager at the mansions of the 'twice-born' elite.

Denial is a basic tenant of such a creed. Denial of rights, denial of opportunities, of justice and fair play etc. gnaw at the vitals of even an autocracy. People's assertion for their basic rights is often met with increased doses of state oppression. Dhritrashtar loved his son. He ignored fair demands of Pandavs for equitable power sharing. He allowed the men around him to indulge in trickery, deceit, strong- arm tactics to divert the Pandavs from their just claim. The situation boiled into the Mahabharat in which the entire Kaurav clan was wiped out in the most gruesome way. Dhritrashtar loved his family so much that he spilled every drop of its blood.

Dhritrashtar's self-inflicted tragedy is beyond compare in the annals of human history. The lessons to be learned from it are obvious. Unfortunately, dynastic politics is invariably and always unable to rise to the obvious. The ache to bequeath legacy dims their sight to the obvious. They would rather gamble and perish, than see and survive. In larger terms, small considerations inflict heavy cost on the value system of a society.

Of all the characters in the Mahabharat, Aswatthama was the only one who was cursed with immortality. He was cursed to live forever in his pain and misery because of the vile act of slaughtering children in the Pandav camp. It was a bona fide mistake --- he had sought to wreck vengeance on the Pandavs for unfairly killing his friend Duryodhan and mistook the sleeping children for the Pandavs. He was sorry for the mistake too. Yet, he was cast into a never ending hell.

Ashwatthama may still be alive somewhere but he slipped out of public memory quickly. In a way, he died ages ago. The real sufferer of the curse, however, is Dhritrashtar. He hasn't faded from social memory. He has lived through the epochs as a cursed example of nepotism. The blind king, not the leprosy- afflicted Ashwatthama, has become immortal. His deed cannot let him die ever.

Power struggle was the hallmark of the Mahabharat. Power and pride led to one after another. Draupadi, in fact, had emerged from the flames of the yagya conducted by Drupad for the purpose of being blessed with a male heir who could kill Dronacharya. The heir was sought to seek revenge against the seer. The purpose of her birth was therefore a war and vengeance.

Draupadi : The Daring Damsel

From a reading of Ved Vyasa's Mahabharat, it is apparent that society in that time was in a state of flux. It was struggling to redefine itself; re-position societal norms and channelize human behavior. The age had been preceded by that of Lord Ram which had firmly decided on the code of personal and social conduct on basis of maryada. Role stereotypes with their ideal templates had also been fixed and adopted by the masses at large. They were, of course, not as exemplary as those prevalent during the preceding era of Satya Yuga in which truth, humanism and integrity reigned supreme.

The Mahabharat era followed the Ramayan era. Many of the accepted norms of the latter had suffered erosion from time and tide. It was therefore time to re-assert Dharma and redefine righteous conduct in the contemporary context.

Like the Ramayan, Mahabharat epic too is dominated by strong, exceptional men and women. Each of them defined a human trait, frail or strong, in their own definitive way since it was believed that each individual had a specific reason to be born and therefore a specific task to perform during its lifetime. There was therefore a story behind the why of birth and another of how the purpose of birth was fulfilled. To be born in a particular class or caste marked the destiny of the person concerned.

Draupadi is an exceptional and the most fascinating character Mahabharat. She was not born in the ordinary way. She rather emerged from the sacred fire, yagya, and was therefore called Yagyaseni. She is therefore fiery and combative; proud of her blood. She also guards her privilege passionately, often insisting on draining the blood out of those who dare to cross her path. Draupadi is an extraordinary women even in an era that was defined by astonishing people.

By the Dwapar era, the age of Lord Krishna, tribal society had became extinct and a feudal set up had been installed. Society was divided in royalty and poverty. The upper caste established its influence and captured the riches. Women too lost their place from the high pedestal of Ramayan days. They became property and lost the independence of their existence. Men owned women and tried to rule them by obtaining them through marriage. Beautiful women were forcibly married as per male whims. Bhisham Pitamah abducted Amba, Ambika and Ambalika for Vichitravirya.

Power struggle was the hallmark of the Mahabharat. Power and pride led to one after another. Draupadi, in fact, had emerged from the flames of the yagya conducted by Drupad for the purpose of being blessed with a male heir who could kill Dronacharya. The heir was sought to seek revenge against the seer. The purpose of her birth was therefore a war and vengeance.

Her story progresses with her marriage to Arjun, who won her hand by piercing the eye of a revolving fish with an arrow in an open contest. Karan was at the contest too. Draupadi was initially attracted to Karan. He was also capable of fulfilling the condition of the contest. But Krishna intervened. Draupadi's marriage to Karan would have upset the purpose for which she was born. He gestured to Draupadi to object to Karan's participation in the contest. After all, he was not of noble birth. He was a charioteer's son. "I won't marry the son of a charioteer," she exclaimed before the royal assembly. Deeply embarrassed by the objection, Karan withdrew from the contest.

Arjun married Draupadi but when she arrived at the hut of the Pandav brothers, their mother, Kunti, unwittingly asked her sons to divide among themselves whatever they had brought home for her. Kunti withdrew her remark later but Draupadi decided to have, not one, but five husbands. She was happy and proud to be the wife of five warriors and often boasted about her unique marital status.

Karan bore Draupadi's insult silently but when the Pandavs lost their wife in a game of dice with the Kaurvs, he retaliated by calling her a 'whore.' He said, "A woman with five husbands cannot but be a whore." Draupadi was livid. The soft corner in her heart for Karan turned into deep hatred.

Karan's comment, however, was in response to the words of caution from Duryodhan's younger sibling, Vikaran. He was the lone voice in the gambling hall where Duryodhan and his friends were heaping insults and taunts on the Pandavs and Draupadi. None of the elders in the assembly had made an effort to silence the Kauravs. Vikaran dared them, saying, "I dare you all, O' kshatriya heroes! Where is your self- respect and regard for the daughter- in- law of this great Kuru race? You all know that it was a premeditated plan and Pandavs have been defeated by cheating. Can anybody answer Panchali's most relevant answer that how Yudhishthir can put her as a stake when he had already lost himself in the game? You are not only quiet on this cheating but you are also quiet to the catastrophe that would follow this hateful sight of Draupadi's insult. Wake up, and save the Kuru race from devastation."

Draupadi herself was infuriated. She wanted her husbands to get her instant revenge for her insult. She also dared the elders and shamed them for their deplorable silence. "I am wife of five warriors and yet insulted. Where is your pride O' great Pandavs. If you fail to take appropriate action then my old father, my brother and my sons would get me justice by killing the Kauravs," she had roared in the hall.

Though Krishna saves her from being completely disrobed, she is incensed enough to take a vow that she would tie her loose hair only after washing them in Dushshasan's blood.

Non-violence was not Draupadi's credo. She believed in violent penal action against the wrong doer. There was no scope for reconciliation or forgiveness with her. During the incognito exile period of the Pandavs, prince Keechak of Virat Nagar kingdom tried to molest her. She demanded instant retribution from her husbands. Yudhishthir tried to convince her that it was not the right time for retribution as it would expose them, and set them on another period of exile. But, she taunted Yudhishthir for his patience. "I have pledged to see him dead before the sun set tomorrow. O' Bheem would you get me my revenge by killing Keechak?" she challenged Bheem knowing his weakness for her.

Similarly, when Hastinapur was on the verge of war and Lord Krishna decided to make a last ditch effort to prevent it, Draupadi confronted him and asked him to desist from it. If there was no war, she asked angrily, how would she redeem her vow of washing her hair in Dushshsan's blood? She couldn't go about unbraided throughout her life.

Draupadi was, in fact, the most bluntly vocal character in the Mahabharat. She articulated her needs and demanded they be met forthwith. She was in a way vain and intemperate. She was proud of having five husbands and also being Abhimanyu's mother, though he was actually Subhadra's child. The biological relationship notwithstanding, Draupadi laid her claim on the lad because her own five children were not as valorous as Abhimanyu.

Despite these aberrations, Draupadi is the most powerful woman character in the Mahabharat. Lord Krishna was on her side. He was her sakha or friend who helped her out of any crisis in her life. She is hailed in the modern discourse as a bold, outspoken woman who could get her way.

The seed of conflict between the Kauravs and the Pandavs were planted by her through an insult early in the story. Duryodhan had come to visit the wondrous palace – the palace of illusions–the Pandavs had created for themselves. He mistook a patch of water for solid ground and fell in the pool. Draupadi had mocked him with the comment, "A blind man's son cannot but be blind." It injured Duryodhan's pride gravely and kicked off the sequence of events later.

Draupadi was indeed a unique privileged woman. She had five husbands but had the privilege of perpetual virginity. Lord Krishna had blessed her with the boon that her maidenhood would be restored after a bath every morning. She therefore could spend one year each with her husbands to deliver their children. But Draupadi was an exception rather than the norm during her time. Polygamy never became an accepted way of life in India.

Though Mahabharat was largely centred around Draupadi's vow for vengeance, she herself and all other women were its biggest victims. Abhimanyu's killing shattered her and it became worse as the wails of widows grew louder as the war progressed. Duryodhan killing was a small personal consolation in a world that was now filled with misery and hopelessness. The war had spared none.On the last day of the war when Draupadi stood in the middle of the battlefield she was left with nothing but grief.

Other prominent women of the epic shared the same fate. Gandhari was tormented by the grief of losing her hundred sons, and her brother Shakuni. Kunti lost Karan while Subhadra had to condole the death of her son Abhimanyu. Uttra fainted after she heard about the death of her husband Abhimanyu. Her womb was also struck by the powerful missile, Brahmastra, shot by Ashwatthama.

In our cultural history, Draupadi is not a dear, venerated name like Sita of Ramayan yug. Sita is loved and respected as an epitome of virtuous womanhood. She was an ideal wife, an ideal mother and an ideal daughter-in-law. Sita achieved a glorious and respectable exit from life when mother earth herself opened up to receive her back into its folds. Draupadi however was left alone when she slipped while trekking with her husbands in the Himalayas on way to heaven. Her five husbands, who she was so proud of, did not bother to cast a backward glance towards her as she fell. Bheem too left her behind. She wailed for her husbands, but in vain. Her death perhaps tellingly marks out what a monumental tragedy was Draupadi's life.

The issue of education as a privilege was rubbed in to a large extent when the story of Mahabharat played on the small screen during the COVID 19 pandemic. It is a well-accepted principle that if you want to learn about a country then you better learn about its educational institutions. Dronacharya's gurukul was largely responsible for introducing education as a privilege. It was designed to nurture dynastic rule. Though such institutions no longer exist, the qualitative difference between government and private colleges make for two different types of schooling. Privatization of education has the feel of Dronacharya's gurukul where imparting education was not a mission but a business.

Dronacharya : The Misguide

The nadir of Adharma in the battle of Mahabharat was plumbed by none other than the Dharmaraj himself. He did so, ironically, in the name of re-establishing Dharma.

The death of Guru Dronacharya was the point in the epic when a dynastic system was ruthlessly destroyed and replaced with another dynastic system. Dronacharya's deceitful death can never be justified. This was against all laws of battle wherein attacking an unarmed person was a sin. The unforgivable death was yet another stain on the Panadavs. They would have never been able to kill Dronacharya or Bhisham or Karan had they not deployed questionable means.

But their sins were said to be pious and were justified in the name of Dharma, and at the instance of God. The deceitful death of Guru Dronacharya proved that system depended on its 'managers' and an able 'manager' could develop his own argument to present wrongdoings in completely different light. Mahabharat is, in fact, the template for perpetuating a dynastic feudal system, sanctioned by the divine incarnation of Lord Krishna.

Mahabharat was the first instance in our mythology where the relationship between the teacher and student was violated. Guru Dronacharya was no ordinary teacher. He wanted to use his students to teach his friend Drupad a lesson for insulting him in his court after he went to him asking for half of his kingdom promised to him in their childhood. The sacred relationship between the guru and shishya was based on a selfish motive in the epic. The sanctity of the relationship was further violated after Dronacharya displayed a marked bias towards some of his students to the detriment of others.

The Acharya secured his interests by aligning with the Kingdom of Hastinapur. He did not side with the Pandavs despite their rightful claim. He was led by his immediate gain from Hastinapur.

He also wanted every luxury for his son Ashwatthama. Such a lifestyle was only possible in the Raj Bhawan of Hastinapur. Dronacharya started an ignoble tradition that patronized the rich and mighty. He supported a system that established exclusive and separate teachings for the privileged and royal princes. He made education a matter of inheritance. It was bestowed on young men on the basis of their birth and caste. It was reverse 'reservation', in a manner of speaking, during Dronacharya's tutelage.

Dronacharya therefore promoted favoritism in the gurukul. Arjun was kept over and above all others. It was actually Acharya's targeted approach to train Arjun in specific fields in order to use him for his own purpose of defeating Drupad. Of course, his acts were rationalized by inserting the theory of the 'grand design' of destiny in the epic. Ironically, Dronacharya was a disciple of Parsuram who had vowed to arm Brahmins so that Kshatriyas were eliminated from the face of earth. The Kshatriya –hater's disciple however served the Kshatriyas all his life. He lived a life full of paradoxes and his teachings too remained embroiled in controversy, especially after he refused to train Karan and Eklavya.

Both Parsuram and Dronacharya can be credited with shackling education to the caste system. They failed to put an equitable teacher-taught ideal before future generations. The adverse impact of their actions continue even to this day.

Interestingly, when the Indian Government decided to re-telecast Mahabharat on Doordarshan, a large chunk of the population was facing the challenge of online instructions. A deadly virus had threatened their lives and livelihood. Educational institutions were closed due to a nationwide lockdown. Students from the lower strata of society did not have access to smart phones or laptops. The government was also in no position to provide at such a massive scale, more so because of the economic slowdown.

The issue of education as a privilege was rubbed in to a large extent when the story of Mahabharat played on the small screen during the COVID 19 pandemic. It is a well-accepted principle that if you want to learn about a country then you better learn about its educational institutions. Dronacharya's gurukul was largely responsible for introducing education as a privilege. It was designed to nurture dynastic rule. Though such institutions no longer exist, the qualitative difference between government and private colleges make for two different types of schooling. Privatization of education has the feel of Dronacharya's gurukul where imparting education was not a mission but a business.

Tragically, under the present system even teachers are chosen. There are accusations that the current regime is promoting a certain ideology while recruiting teachers. It is also allegedly destroying institutions which have a different point of view from the government. Dronacharya chose his students, and when he decided to train Arjun as the best archer in the world, nothing could stop him. He handpicked his students for imparting certain skills, and deprived others with the same talent of his guidance.

Dronacharya vainly guided his son Ashwatthama to choose his friends too because he knew that in the ultimate war between the Kauravs and Pandavs, it would be the Pandavs who would win. Hence, he wanted to secure his son's future with them but Ashwatthama was friends with Duryodhan and his brothers because of their riches. Ashwatthama had spent his childhood in deprivation and preferred to enjoy a luxurious life with them.

Dronacharya had the unique characteristic that he picked the best students and left the others to their own fate. He made no effort to groom the errant in a better way of life. He avoided reforming Duryodhan and instead chose an obedient Arjun to be his favorite. He had his moment when he could have earned the reverence as a teacher in the eyes of the generations to come by accepting Eklavya as his pupil. He should have embraced Eklavya for the very fact that he was learning by erecting his statute. He, instead, saw his low caste and deprived him of his guidance. He also saw a great danger for Arjun in the skill of Eklavya and did something that did not behoove a teacher. He blatantly asked for Eklavya's thumb as his guru dakshina.

There was a basic difference between Parsuram and Dronacharya. Dronacharya suffered miseries in his early life. He was so poor that his wife had to mix flour with water and offer it to her son Ashwatthama as milk. Dronacharya couldn't bear the deprivation and he approached his childhood friend Drupad for help. Drupad insulted him and destroying Drupad became Dronacharya's aim in life.

A Brahmin, who was suffering despite his education, therefore, decided to teach Kshatriyas the skills of warfare. He had realized that a union of authority and weaponry can win him anything that is required for a luxurious life. A starved and deprived Dronacharya became an empowered Dronacharya

Thus, an unholy nexus between Brahmins and Kshatriyas was formed to decide who would and who would not be educated. The nexus handpicked students as can be illustrated by the examples of four characters of Karan, Eklavya, Ashatthama and Arjun. Eklavya and Karan were left out. Ashwatthama was admitted into the royal gurukul because he was the teacher's son. Karan and Eklavya did not suit the ultimate goal of Dronacharya and were rejected on trivial considerations. Dronacharya had the great opportunity to reform the then existing highly partisan education system but he failed the test miserably.

However, Dronacharya had foreseen the future. He had told Arjun that his dharma was to fight even if he was standing against him. He knew that he would have to pay the price of remaining with the Kauravs due to his obvious considerations. His poverty and affection for his son compelled him to take asylum with Kauravs. He repaid the favor by fighting against the Pandavs in the great war, but not before declaring that he would not kill any of the five brothers. He was especially inclined towards Arjun. It was for the sake of establishing Arjun's dominance in battlefield that he treated Eklavya and Karan in a partisan manner.

Lord Krishna and his elder brother Balaram wanted that education should reach everybody desirous of it. The brothers were shining examples of education unindered by caste considerations.

They knew it was the foundation of empowerment and hence did not feel it right to deprive anybody of its benefits. The feudal system intentionally kept the deprived sections and women out of the gurukuls. Dronacharya's death in the war, by a deceitful act of his student Yudishthir, was needed in the epic to show the flaws of the prevailing gurukul system.

In modern India, reservation is a strong means to end discrimination and take education to the deprived sections of society. But it is not that easy to end discrimination. We still have institutions that are exclusively for the rich and the privileged. The privatisation of education from Nursery to the University level promotes this exclusive and special treatment. Even if someone gets admission in these institutions after the country introduced the right to education act which provides certain percentage of seats for the economically weaker section, it is not easy to survive in an otherwise hostile atmosphere. Modern education system is still in the clutches of a feudal system. Had it not been so, there would not have been an exclusive school reserved for the children of senior officers of Government of India.

Ironically, the Indian system seems inclined to foster the tradition of the gurukuls. Had it not been so, Haryana would not have changed the name of Gurgaon to Gurugram after Dronacharya. In the history books of Haryana schools, Gurgaon is shown as the workplace of Dronacharya. The Dronacharya award in the name of Dronacharya too proves our governments' obsession with its traditional symbols.

Guru Dronacharya's major weakness was his son and he died because of his affection for him. When he heard the false news of his son's death from Yudhishthir, he laid down his weapons and Dhrishtdyuman beheaded him. Yudhishthir had the dubious distinction of being the first messenger of fake news. Dronacharya's son Ashwatthama was blessed with immortality, his father too became immortal because of the education system he had initiated during his lifetime.

Black hats of our mythological narration are verily complicated. They have deeply impacted our history, culture and lifestyle because there is always a certain glamour attached to them. Mahabharat has an atypical characteristic that its villains are so complex that at certain points the reader starts fitting them into the frame of the hero. He is so filled with a number of good qualities that are described in such enormity of the character that the reader starts considering him a hero despite his acts of omission and commission.

The Dilemma of Duryodhan

Black hats of our mythological narration are verily complicated. They have deeply impacted our history, culture and lifestyle because there is always a certain glamour attached to them. Mahabharat has an atypical characteristic that its villains are so complex that at certain points the reader starts fitting them into the frame of the hero. Duryodhan was one such villain. He is so filled with a number of good qualities that are described in such enormity of the character that the reader starts considering him a hero despite his acts of omission and commission.

He was valorous and full of himself. He had a unique quality of friendship. He was, in fact, asserting his right to succeed his father, King Dhritrashtar.

When he was killed in the end by deceit, like his friend Karan, his Guru Dronacharya, and his brother-in-law Jaidarath, the reader starts to look at him as a defeated, unfortunate hero. In a number of discourses, he is therefore either named Suyodhan or it is recommended that he be called Suyodhan. He steals the show after he is deceitfully killed by Bheem at the behest of none other than Lord Krishna. He is one character of Mahabharat that is deeply entrenched in a dilemma from the beginning to the end --- to be good or to be bad.

Mahabharat is not just a story of the fiercest battle of our ancient past. It is instead a supreme message on Dharma delivered by Lord Krishna. He conveyed the reason why he took the human form. "I incarnate when righteousness (Dharma) declines and unrighteousness (Adharma) becomes rampant. I then come down to earth to protect and strengthen the Dharma and punish the wicked," Krishna tells an anxious Arjun who had declined to fight his own brothers, uncles, teachers, etc. This particular verse of Mahabharat is not that easy to understand. It lays the foundation for the enunciation of a supreme principle.

We interpret this shloka in the light of the circumstances but not in a generic fashion or literally. What was the ultimate gain in this encounter of good and bad? How did our society benefits from it? The answer is not simple. One has to consider it in specific terms and within a timeframe.

Picture this: The battlefield of Kurukshetra is full of dead bodies. Vultures are all over the sky and widows, mothers and sisters are wailing at their loss. They are not common women. They include the queen of Hastinapur Gandhari, who lost 99 sons. Her severely wounded hundredth son was hiding somewhere waiting for his imminent death. Kunti, who lost her eldest son Karan and her grandson Abhimanyu, Subhadra who lost her son, a pregnant Uttara who lost her husband and got her unborn son hurt in her womb, are also deeply grieved. But these names are of those who ultimately got something out of this war–Hastinapur and its powerful regime. Thousands of other women too lost their sons, husbands, fathers, brothers and other relatives for no apparent gain. Instead, miseries of life in the post war scenario were bequeathed to them.

Duryodhan, at the instance of Lord Krishna, was hit below the belt by Bheem. Gandhari had converted his body into steel, barring his upper thigh and waist. Krishna knew of the blessing since it was on his advice that Duryodhan had covered his shame before his mother. He gets the sympathy of the reader since he had been incapacitated by the use of unfair means. There was no glory in Bheem's victory.

Duryodhan's character defined the rules of royalty and ambition to retain power by hook or crook. Because of him, Krishna came face to face with Shakuni. Both had their own definition and justification of what constituted Dharma and Adharma.

Duryodhan's father Dhritrashtar was denied the crown when his brother Vidur ruled him out due to his blindness. "A handicap is not worthy of the crown. Hence, I strongly advise not to crown Dhritrashtar as the king." The other brother Pandu became the king. He soon abdicated and left for the forest for austerity and penance. Dharitrashtar was re-installed. Consequently, Duryodhan claimed the crown as his natural right to succeed his father. Pandu's sons, the Pandavs, had their own claim to the inheritance.

Dhritrashtar was a deeply complexed personality largely because of his handicap. The blindness made him determined that only his lineage was perpetuated in the kingdom of Hastinapur. His wife Gandhari too suffered from a similar complex. She was cursed by her husband for not being able to bear him an heir before Pandu's wife Kunti had a child. In a way, Duryodhan was in competition with Yudhishthir even before his birth.

The Kauravs are natural sons of Dhritrashtar and Gandhari, whereas the Pandavs were born through the intervention of various gods. They were not related by blood to their father Pandu. Duryodhan had therefore insisted that they had no right to the crown since they were not his biological off-springs.

Pandavs were of the opinion that Dhritrashtar was ruling in the name of Pandu and hence they had a rightful claim to the crown. In Mahabharat, the question of succession became complex immediately after Shantanu married Satyawati. In the script of Mahabharat, Dharma was decided by the one who had gained power by any means. Legitimacy of power was flexible and molded as per requirement by the one who had captured it. Mahabharat, in fact, shows us how to look at Dharma from the window of the palace. Duryodhan, and prior to him Shantanu, viewed Dharma from the perch of their palace.

Satyawati's condition for marrying to Shantanu was that her son should be his successor. She wanted to perpetuate her lineage in the ruling class, ignoring the right of the eldest son Bhisham. Blind by his love, Shantanu agreed to the terms and pushed Hastinapur on the war path.

However, if a father was handicapped, blind as in the case of Dhritrashtar, then his son would also be deprived of the crown despite the fact that he was sitting on the throne but only representing Pandu. Effectively, it meant that a handicap can rule but as a representative. Not as a full-fledged authority. His son might be fully physically fit but would not succeed to the throne because he was son of a representative of the original claimant.

Similarly, if the king was blind then his wife too lost her right to see the colours of life. Hence, Gandhari covered her eyes with a band after her marriage to Dhritrashtar. The feudal system kept women at a weaker position. Gandhari was an ideal wife because she blindly obeyed the feudal doctrine. A woman who dreamed of being bigger than her husband or saw more than her husband was considered a threat to the patriarchal system. But if she deprive herself of the same physical faculty which her husband was suffering from then she turned into a Sati (chaste woman). Gandhari filled herself and her son with a darkness under which Duryodhan became a mere pawn in the hands of Gandhari's brother Shakuni who had vowed to destroy Hastinapur.

From his father Dhritrashtar to his uncle Shakuni, everyone poisoned Duryodhan's upbringing. He was convinced that the Pandavs were his enemies since they would deprive him of his crown. The subsequent conflict over succession became so vicious that it led to the Mahabharat.

From the medieval to the Mughal times, sons killed their fathers and brothers killed their brothers to seize power. The trend was not confined to India only. It was prevalent worldwide in various monarchies and autocracies. It had led to the birth of the most common adage, `Everything is fair in love and war.' Rules were bent to suit the incumbent and to prevent the next. This was precisely the case in Mahabharat. Pandavs were interpreting the rules of rule to suit them whereas the Kauravs elucidated them to retain control.

Krishna entered the Mahabharat to establish Dharma. His righteousness was such that whosoever was given a place by his side, he or she automatically became righteous. Draupadi and Arjun were two such examples. On the other side, whosoever challenged Krishna or anybody associated with him, was deemed a practitioner of Adharma, unrighteousness. An attack below the belt was considered a grave and punishable violation, but in the case of Duryodhan, Krishna, the Lord himself, provoked Bheem to hit Duryodhan below the waist. It led to his gruesome and painful death. "Unrighteous ways to establish righteousness are justified. You should not hesitate in your action to establish Dharma. I have come down to earth to establish Dharma. I am in all and all are in me," Krishna told Arjun, and thus justified Adharma for the sake of Dharma.

Balram who taught war- craft to both Duryodhan and Bheem got annoyed after Bheem unabashedly violated the rules of the one-on-one combat. "I will always be embarrassed that I taught you, O Bheem. You have brought such a shame to my name by violating the rules of the combat that was being held under my watch. I curse you. I would always be proud of my pupil Duryodhan whom you would never have defeated had you not attacked him against the rules," Balaram said before leaving Kurukshetra. But his eulogy of Duryodhan could not prevent him from dying a lonely and dreadful death.

Duryodhan's death proved that the ultimate goal was to gain power, and, if the end of a war was a victory then all legitimate-illegitimate means adopted to gain it were justified.

Friendships were sacrosanct for Duryodhan. He held Karan as his best friend and continued his friendship with him till the end. Ashwatthama was also passionately devoted to him. Post Mahabharat analysis of the epic, glorified him for certain qualities. He was the perfect anti-hero, or perhaps a tragic hero.

Duryodhan's character also resonates in its tragedy with the readers when his commanders Bhisham Pitamah and Dronacharya prays for the victory of Pandavs while fighting on the side of Duryodhan. Both of them had taken a pledge not to kill any of the Pandavs. Even his friend Karan had promised his mother Kunti, who went to him asking for the life of her sons, that he won't kill four of her five sons. "I promise you that I won't kill four of your five sons but I cannot give you the same promise about Arjun. However, if one of us dies, you still be mother of five sons," he told Kunti on the margins of the battlefield. True to his words, he avoided killing four Pandavs though they came within his reach.

At the end, a reader is left with a message that evil was dead with the death of Duryodhan. But had he been killed without any deceit, it would have been a larger message for the mankind and nobody would have empathised with the dying villain. Ironically, though Krishna labeled him as a villain, he also opened a window of sympathy for him through his deceitful death. Bheem takes only a pusillanimous contentment in his death and is disliked when the curtains fall on the battle.

It is said that `One man's villain is another man's hero` and Mahabharat manifested the theory in the most magnificent way. All villains or heroes, unknown to them, nurture a Duryodhan inside them. We are heroes and villains simultaneously. A Duryodhan lives within us all the time despite our protestations to the contrary.

Gandhari's decision to cover her eyes has been interpreted in many different ways. There are a number of for and against arguments over her decision. It has been said that darkness in her life is representative of the repression of women in the feudal set up. The repression continues in the present time too. Women, who suppress themselves for the sake of a happy marriage, nurture frustration and depression. The suppressed anger explodes at a later stage and destroys families.

Gandhari : The Banded Queen

Everyone embraces a new bright life in marriage but not Gandhari. She instead wrapped herself in darkness for the sake of her husband Dhritrashtar's blindness. The young and exuberant princess of Gandhar had not been given the option of swayamvar (the practice to choose one's husband from a number of royal suitors). She was rather offered the non-rejectable proposal of marriage by the most feared and venerated warrior of the time, the Bhisham Pitamah.

There was no kingdom that could have afforded to reject a proposal of marriage from Hastinapur. Her parents though were skeptical about her future and were yet contemplating an answer when Gandhari agreed in order to avoid any standoff between the two countries.

She accepted the marriage to blind Dhritrashtar as her destiny and covered her eyes by a tying a piece of cloth over them in order to express her commitment to her husband. Her action was by no means less than Bhisham's vow of celibacy. The feudal lords of the time unfortunately made no effort to prevent her from doing so. They instead hailed her as a sati (a woman unconditionally devoted to her husband).

Gandhari was another complex Mahabharat character. The strip on her eyes is actually a symbol of resistance. It was resistance against the forced marriage in a feudal system. She did not protest openly but over time burned herself in the fire of retribution.

Her band reminds everybody of a rotten system where even the God deceived her of her genuine wish to save her hundredth son, Duryodhan. She was shattered after Bheem slaughtered her 99 sons in battle. She wanted to save the remaining one from his imminent death at the hands of Bheem. She wanted to transfer the accumulated energy of her penance to him. She sent a message to Duryodhan to come in front of her without any clothes. "A mother knows her children from their childhood and does everything for them. So don't be shy and conceal yourself from my first sight since my marriage. O` dear son, let me protect you from death." Gandhari's message was clear but Lord Krishna's deliberate taunt led Duryodhan to cover his loins.

The woman, who had preserved her all energies and emotions, including anger, was deeply aggrieved by Krishna's mischief. Duryodhan's body was turned into steel by Gandhari's glance, save for the covered part of the body. It became his Achilles' heel. She cursed Krishna after Duryodhan's killing with dying a lonely death and the total annihilation of the Yadav clan.

Gandhari was the most powerful character of Mahabharat. It's understandable that she did not get her fair share of glory as she was not on the Lord's side, the side of the righteous. She was however given the greatest honour of the time and she was placed in the company of great women of our mythology that included Lakshmi, Parvati, Sita, Mandodari, and Ahilya.

Her character opens up a number of doors to various ancient and modern narratives because of her voice of resistance. She was the only woman character of the epic to challenge Lord Krishna, the creator of the universe, for his partisan inclination towards the Pandavs and the trickery to ensure that Kauravs were routed in the war. "You could have changed the course of destiny and saved this war but you did not and hence I am left devastated. You took my last son too from me. O'Lord, why?" she questioned Krishna after he misguided Duryodhan to wear a piece of cloth around his waist. Lord Krishna smiled at her outburst because it was not him, rather destiny, that had played its due role.

Gandhari was a picture of strength amid her trials and tribulations. No character matched her suffering. She was the only one in Hastinapur to have exclusive right over suffering from her self-imposed blindness to bearing the loss of a hundred sons. Druapadi, who has been eulogized in majority of post Mahabharat narratives, appears like a dwarf before her sacrifice and poise. Unlike Draupadi, she was neither revengeful nor remorseless. After she cursed Lord Krishna in her misery and self-pity, she immediately apologized to him for her intemperate behavior. She wanted him to allow her to take back her curse or suggest an antidote to it. If you want to evaluate Gandhari against the other women characters, think of Kunti who caused the death of her eldest son Karan at the hands of her younger and preferred son Arjun, and Draupadi, who soaked her hair in the blood of Dushshasan right in the middle of the battlefield of Kurukshetra with innumerable dead bodies of soldiers strewn around her.

Unlike Gandhari, we have Amba in Mahabharat who marked Bhisham Pitamah after he refused to marry her due to his vow of celibacy. Bhisham had abducted Amba to wed Vichitravirya. But she was in love with Salva and had chosen him as her husband. After Bhisham got to know about it, he freed Amba. Salva refused to accept her because of a grudge against Bhisham. A distraught Amba went back to Bhisham and pleaded with him to marry her but Bhisham was bound by his word. Even Vichitravirya refused to marry her as her heart had been with somebody else.

She then wanted revenge on Bhisham and requested a number of princes and kings to kill Bhisham but no one had the courage to take on Bhisham, the greatest warrior of his time. Moved by her grief, Parsuram dared Bhisham to a one- on- one combat but their long drawn battle remained inconclusive. A hopeless Amba turned to the Himalayas and performed rigorous penance. When Lord Shiva appeared before her, she asked him for Bhisham's death. Shiva granted her the boon that she would cause Bhisham's death in her next birth. She was thereafter born as Shikhandi, and had she not gone an extra mile to fulfill her vow, the result of Mahabharat would have been different. She was the only one woman in Mahabharat who actively participated in the war and bayed for the blood of the most outstanding combatant of the Kuru race.

But there was no revenge or ill will in Gandhari's heart. She was not blind by birth but made her choice after marrying the blind Dhritrashtar. Though Gandhari accepted her fate willingly, she was an example of a forced and unmatched marital alliance.

Gandhari had exemplary endurance. She knew that her sons were fighting a losing battle but she controlled herself and at no time disturbed her relations with her sister- in- law Kunti. The game of dice opened a wound in her heart it festered through the story because it was her brother who was directing the action in the palace sitting beside her son. She gave a fair try to stop the war, including intervening with Lord Krishna, but her efforts did not yield the desired results.

Her resolve remained weak as her position in Hastinapur was far from a commanding one. Her father had compromised by agreeing to her marriage, while her brother had taken an oath to destroy the family that she was wedded to. Shakuni was actually quite an antithesis of a brother. Brothers usually do everything possible to ensure the happiness of their sister. Shakuni wanted the exact opposite. His victory through trickery in the game of dice laid the foundation of a war that destroyed the Kuru clan completely. It killed him, too.

Gandhari remained impartial till the death of her ninety nine sons. She had blessed both the Kauravs and Pandavs equally, a feat no one could have matched, including family elders like Bhisham and Dronacharya. They were fighting from the side of Duryodhan but had given their blessings to the Pandavs. Duryodhan asked Bhisham, "Grandsire, why have you not blessed me victory? Don't you think that my victory would be your victory?" Bhisham told him, "O'Duryodhan, you can seek blessing but cannot choose them. It remains the right of the giver. For you, I wish a long age." The answer indicated the result of the war in full measure.

Gandhari was remarkable in another way. Unlike Kunti, who reached out to her discarded son Karan to seek his favour for her five sons, Gandhari did not knock on any door for Duryodhan. In the end, she herself decided to transfer her accumulated energy to him. It makes her stand apart from other female characters of Mahabharat. She had empowered herself enough to make her son undefeatable. She was however deceived by Krishna.

Gandhari's decision to cover her eyes has been interpreted in many different ways. There are a number of for and against arguments over her decision. It has been said that darkness in her life is representative of the repression of women in the feudal set up. The repression continues in the present time too. Women, who suppress themselves for the sake of a happy marriage, nurture frustration and depression. The suppressed anger explodes at a later stage and destroys families.

In other words, the failure to protest at the appropriate time can only lead to suffering and misery later on. The band on Gandhari's eyes is symbolic of the fact that if women do not set their own and keep their eyes wide open, they are in for a disaster.

When Mahabharat was shown on national broadcaster Doordarshan and Draupadi appeared in a glamorous avatar and was called a `whore` by Karan in the gambling hall of Hastinapur, Karan became a villain instantly. But when a high-born proud Draupadi insulted Karan by calling him Soot Putra, she was praised for standing her ground. It became an example of woman empowerment. In a way, it was the feudal system speaking in a modern voice.

Karan : The Ultimate Warrior

The biggest challenge before mankind in the twenty first century is one of identity. The great seer Ved Vyasa created a hero in Karan but in the entire epic he was caught in a Chakravyuh of identity because of the lie related to his birth. He is vulnerable and degraded in the narration because of the lie of his low birth.

Karan was a victim of false identity that turned him into a defeated villain from an initial hero. His entry in the epic is so grand and powerful that he puts its hero Arjun on the back foot when the latter was to display his proficiency in archery. A little before it, Kuru princes were showing their expertise in their favourite weapons and entire stadium echoed with victory chants for Arjun. But as soon as Arjun readied himself, Karan stepped in.

Karan's appearance in his divine breast shield and golden earrings stunned the gathering. He became their favorite instantly. The challenge to Arjun was not only unexpected but serious too. Hastinapur's raj guru Kripacharya and the teacher of Kuru princes` Dronacharya hastily intervened to save the day for Arjun. They demanded his identity.

Karan was not a prince and was hence disqualified. Duryodhan gave him a kingdom instantly. He was now qualified. The gurus then threw an ace. They asked him to reveal his parentage. Karan did not hide the fact that he was not of noble birth but was a charioteer's son. He was disqualified by reasons of his low caste birth. Karan, despite being snubbed in public over his parentage, became a hero in the early part of the epic.

He appears as a potential hero again at Draupadi's swayamvar. He was ready to take on Arjun in the contest to win the princess' hand. But she called him out by his caste name and refused his candidature. Karan silently suffered the insult but gave vent to his feelings against Draupadi when he called her a prostitute at the time of cheer haran. The remark turned him from a hero to a villain.

Sage Ved Vyasa had declared about his epic that what did not exist in Mahabharat, it did not exist in Bharat. Vyasa's claim is largely true because characters like Karan have been viewed from multiple angles in Bharat. In his modern day epic, Rashmirathi, Ramdhari Singh Dinkar attacked the caste system through him. Karan's identity was established with a lie at the time of his birth. He was Kunti's illegitimate child. His foster mother was Radha and was affectionately called Radhey. Kunti had floated him down the river because she feared that a child before marriage would jeopardize her prospects with King Pandu.

The creator of Mahabharat had decided its heroes and Karan was not among them. He was therefore denied the chance to compete with Arjun at the Hastinapur stadia. The test of parentage was applied to Karan but the Pandavs were exempted from it. It was common knowledge that Pandu wasn't the biological father of any of them. Duryodhan raised the issue when he taunted Bheem for questioning Karan's credentials. ``We too have heard a lot of stories of your own origin, brother Bheem. Better let them not be told or a number of us would be embarrassed."

He then made a fervent appeal to allow Karan to compete on the ground that valour was the only quality of a warrior and it was not good to deny him this chance to prove himself on the basis of the meaningless reason of caste. "There are hundreds of examples where people from humble origins made to greater achievements, occupied top positions and were praised than shamed on such a flimsy ground." But Duryodhan's exhortations were ignored by the kul gurus and family elders.

Ved Vyas turned Karan's personality into that of a daanvir, the epitome of charity, but refused him the glory of the greatest warrior of his time. The narrative thereafter flows accordingly. His teacher Parsuram's curse of forgetting his skills at the most critical juncture in the epic battle ultimately caused his death. The then prevailing patriarchal system made him an instrument to justify the arrangement where valour and heroism was only reserved for the royalty and upper caste Kshatriyas. It established that it was only the Kshatriya who can fight and kill; move the wheel of history as per the tenants of the feudal system.

The system, in fact, was heavily depended on physical survival and the battlefields determined who was fit enough to survive. Ved Vyas painted a detailed word-picture of feudal Bharat in Mahabharat and Karan was not suited for its appropriate portrayal. But he wanted to give Karan his due also. And since he wanted to introduce India with a hero that is loved, sympathised and praised, he concealed Karan's origin and made him a symbol of a caste system. Karan was killed by Arjun in a deceitful manner, helped also by the curse by Brahamin Parsuram, but he shone as a brave warrior in the battle. Interestingly, in the final act, Karan garners all sympathies and comes out as the hero while Arjun cannot help but be the perpetuator of a villainous action. Arjun victory over Karan emerged as a defeat of his ethics as a warrior and as king.

Tragically, every character in Mahabharat questioned Karan's caste, including Lord Krishna. As a matter of fact, it was at the behest of Krishna that Draupadi refused to allow Karan, son of a charioteer, to participate in her royal swayamvar. Krishna is the key figure of the entire epic and everything either revolves around him or is moved by him. In the battlefield, Krishna was a charioteer himself. Though it was a symbolic act to show that it was Krishna who drives the universe, but this was not the case with Karan. The charioteer tag dogged him repeatedly and he had to suffer consequences of his 'illegitimate' birth.

The feudal system was so strong that his real mother Kunti, despite having identified him, refused to accept him publically in the arena where he challenged Arjun and pledged to kill him. Kunti remained a mute spectator thus losing yet another chance to own him as her son. She was perpetually afraid of losing her position in the royal family.

When Mahabharat was shown on national broadcaster Doordarshan and Draupadi appeared in a glamorous avatar and was called a `whore` by Karan in the gambling hall of Hastinapur, Karan became a villain instantly. But when a high-born proud Draupadi insulted Karan by calling him Soot Putra, she was praised for standing her ground. It became an example of woman empowerment. In a way, it was the feudal system speaking in a modern voice.

Karan's voice in opposition and protest though still survives and gives strength to hundreds and thousands of those who are struggling against the stigma of caste and want to come out of it by excelling in their own field.

Mahabharat and Ramayan are two epics that bring Bharat and Bharatwasis together. Their verses make India a union with all its diversity. From North to South and from East to West, these epics and their stories effect lives of Indians. They are reference points of Indian life and provide the context of day-to-day conduct and value system. The connect of the epics and their characters have not dimmed over the centuries of their telling and re-telling through both ancient and modern media.

While the Ramayan is an episcopal expression of morality, transparency, honesty and character, the Mahabharat is the song of death and Karma. It stings the reader with the reality of death and exhorts him to work selflessly with no expectations. It inspires towards selfless action, Dharma and good Karma.

The message of the Mahabharat, and more specifically the Gita, showed its contemporary relevance during the deadly pandemic of 2020-2021 when death gripped the world in its deadly claws. It reduced humans to a whimpering mass before the onslaught of nature. Powerful leaders stood helplessly as death harvested a large portion of the global population in one fell swoop. The illusion of human might was shattered to bits.

Mahabharat provided succor to mankind amidst its worst-ever health crisis and the subsequent dance of death. Its telecast also brought to the fore several questions. Does the world really needs the great theory of selfless Karma to survive? Or the action to contain the deadly virus? How would have the lakhs of people who undertook the journey home on foot amidst want and poverty from their workplaces survived if they had reconciled with their fate and accepted death in strange faraway places? The government too needed to take its own lesson from the great epic and should have lent a strong hand of support to the hapless victims like Lord Krishna who provided Draupadi enough provisioning out of a single grain of leftover rice when Sage Durvasa visited her home. We also needed to take inspiration from Karan and fight for our rights amid all odds?

A number of critics try to draw Karan's parallel in Homer's Odyessy's immortal hero Achilles. They did indeed have a number of things in common–from their God- like appearance to their unmatched valour and swordsmanship–but when it comes to their life purpose the two differ. Achilles fought for his own personal glory while Karan fought for his self- respect and prestige.

Karan was a strong medium by which Ved Vyas denounced the caste system even as he extensively reported on it. Perhaps, he believed in it too. He could have rooted Karan's origin in the royal family, concealed it in the beginning and revealed it at the most crucial juncture in the battlefield of Kurukshetra. Despite the writer's shrewd twist, Karan emerged as the strongest warrior against the curse of the caste system and still continues to engage us with his deeds.

The crisis of identity, however, remains the hall mark of Karan's character. It can be seen in contemporary times in its worst form post 2014 when the first full- majority Bharatiya Janata Party government took over under the leadership of Narendra Modi and a deadly virus hit the world in 2019, the year of Modi's second coming. He had emerged stronger in electoral terms but this time he made the individual much more important than the system. Politics, and even the democracy, suffered miserably because of politics of identity, even as the virus hit almost every household of the country.

Everyone was then trying to find ways and means to deal with the virus but they failed to do so. Those who had grown larger than the system were the most vulnerable and the people of the country had no choice other than to suffer the consequences of a a pandemic. Karan typifies the current common man who is trying to find his own self in the feudal system but is surrounded by deceit, cheating and treachery.

People also try to draw parallel between Karan and Vibhishnan of Ramayan. Both are on thin ice when analysed as a hero or as a villain. One has to struggle to judge who was making the right selection when it came to taking the side of truth and morality.

Karan was under obligation of Duryodhan since he had given him identity when he needed it the most. It was another matter that it failed to give him any advantage in fighting with Arjun. Vibhishan, on the other hand, preferred Lord Rama in place of his brother who had abducted Sita thus committing an act that was judged as immoral. However, if Karan is looked upon from the perspective of a woman, he stood by Duryodhan who was responsible for Draupadi's disrobing. The action was immoral and self-serving as Karan's sole concern was to ingratiate himself with Duryodhan. He was repaying the debt of his friend for giving him self- respect and authority at a time when others were shaming him.

Despite the warts, Karan is respected and loved in every household of the country. People name their child after him. Vibhishnan, on the other hand, finds no such favor. Vibhishan example is held out in a negative way as `ghar ka bhedi Lanka dhaye' --- as one who can sabotage one's one family.

Mythological epics generally place God at the centre of their tale, and whoever is on the who's side wins. In Mahabharat, Krishna is with Pandavs and hence their immorality is also coated in morality and considered genuine. Duryodhan does not have the same luxury as he fails to choose the Lord to be on his side. But Karan was unmoved. His commitment was different than Bhisham who was tied up with Kauravs because of his oath to the throne. It was a feudalistic choice. Karan's choice was on account of emotional reasoning and gratitude. His identity was driven from his exemplary commitment and every reader wants to be like him in commitment.

Karan as well as Vibhishan faced an identity crisis in crucial moments of their life. Arjun had one too but Krishna delivered the divine message to him in the middle of the battlefield. Karan did not have this privilege, and despite his superior valour and stronger commitment, he fell. Arjun was fated to be a hero as he was chosen by Krishna. In the same manner Vibhishan was Lord Rama's chosen one.

Karan, in fact, emerges from the epic as one who was wronged by his peers under the watch of God. His character demands his share of heroism, which had been usurped by a person who broke every rule in the book to mark himself as a hero. Karan's life is, in many ways, a telling commentary on the feudal system and its tragic consequences.

Mahabharat is deeply entrenched in dynastic pride. Though women had no place on the throne as a matter of right yet, they were the ones who nurtured the feudal structure by bearing male heirs to the throne in order to become 'proud mothers' and presiding queens in the dynastic set up.

Kunti : Karma

Mahabharat is deeply entrenched in dynastic pride. Though women had no place on the throne as a matter of right yet, they were the ones who nurtured the feudal structure by bearing male heirs to the throne in order to become 'proud mothers' and presiding queens in the dynastic set up.

Women who want to fashion an ideal by their lifestyle and strict adherence of their expected role, end up falling prey to a curse that too by a fellow woman only. Mahabharat's story plot is actually a bunch of paradoxes. Kunti, who bore her publically declared eldest son, Yudhishthir, had a child from an earlier illicit relationship too. She had abandoned Karan and went on to marry Pandu, the heir to the Kuru dynasty. Kunti's act of 'Adharma' sets the ball rolling for events that led to the tragedy of Mahabharat.

But Kunti was not the first one to have a child away from the sacrament of marriage. Her grandmother-in-law Satyawati had one too from Rishi Parashar. The child of their mystical union was Ved Vyas, the author of Mahabharat. Satywati however did not shy away from the fact of virgin birth. She candidly and proudly admitted to it. Satyawati by her decision to speak out became the proud mother of the greatest figure of her time, whereas Kunti soaked herself in frustration and despair by concealing the birth of the greatest warrior and marking him for an ignominious death for him. It was an indelible stain on her motherhood.

Kunti failed to muster courage to follow in her footsteps. She concealed the fact as she was afraid of losing her status as a royal queen. The lack of honesty later created a sequence of events which annihilated the Kuru clan. Lord Krishna's words sound truer in this context. He told Kunti's son Arjun in the Gita, "Nobody ain't doing nothing. It's Me. All the world has emanated from Me and would absorb in Me. You are merely pawns in the hands of destiny. So hey Arjun, waiver thee not and follow the path of Karma. Leave it to me to decide the fate of the mankind and virtues and iniquities of the world."

So before we proceed on Kunti and her Karma, we need to know in definite terms that the creator of Mahabharat, the great seer Ved Vyas was himself born through Niyog (a birth without any physical contact). The author had himself born with a definitive purpose. After the death of Chitrangad and Vichitravirya, Bhisham refused to marry because of his oath of celibacy. There was a power vacuum with no heir to the throne.

At this juncture, Satyawati, without the fear of the moral backlash, unhesitatingly declared that she was the mother of Ved Vyas. "I am proud to announce that I bore great seer Ved Vyas in my womb. I was privileged to be chosen for it before my marriage to receive the seed of the fountainhead of knowledge in me by Sage Parashar," Significantly, she did not do so under any fear or duress but declared it of her own volition. She was unlike Kunti.

Her entry into the epic is grand for she was not an ordinary woman. She was exceedingly beautiful who was so full of virtues that Sage Durvasa, who would curse someone over even a minor provocation, blessed her with the power to summon any God to co-habit with her. Kunti, in her curiosity decided to test the effectiveness of the boon and summoned the Sun God. He immediately appeared before her. Kunti was flabbergasted and was afraid to take the next step as it would land her in trouble. She implored Surya Dev, "O God, I am so blessed to have seen you. I thank you for this kind gesture but now I request you to please go back. I do not want any more of this visit."

But the Sun God said that as per Sage Durvasa's boon he could not go back without putting his seed in her womb through Niyog. He then blessed her with his seed. Kunti was devastated. She was the princess and if she became an unmarried mother it would stain the family forever. Though the boon was of Durvasa and fetus was of the Sun and both of them could have been summoned again to clarify on her behalf but Kunti wasn't willing to go that far. She decided to discard her child and failed to pioneer a new and strong role for the woman in society. She, instead of standing up, preferred to be confined in the prevailing system of patriarchy. Her action meant that a woman was merely a fertile ground for providing an heir in the feudal structure.

Ironically, Pandu was cursed by a sage, who he had killed during his moments of intimacy with his wife. The curse was that Pandu would die immediately as he made physical contact with his wives again. The curse became a blessing in disguise for Kunti. Seeing her husband in a state of despair, Kunti confided in him the boon of sage Durvasa. Pandu urged her to summon the gods as he wanted to have children. Thus, Kunti gave birth to Yudhishthir, Bheem and Arjun, and his other wife Madri to Nakul and Sahdev. The wheel of destiny moved a full circle for her and Durvasa's blessing became a boon for the feudal authority. Though Pandu had happily accepted the boon of Durvasa and Kunti had an ideal moment to share the birth of Karan with him, she did not do so.

Kunti was afraid of a system which did not stigmatize an incapable Pandu but shamed women who would gave birth out of wedlock. It was an unpardonable act even if the woman was a princess or a queen. She was an independent entity in the eyes of society. She rather was a representative of her husband. Kunti, with her divine power, not only gave birth to three sons but gave two sons to her husband's second wife too.

In the stadia, when Karan challenged Arjun, Kunti immediately recognized Karan but by that time she had become the widow of Pandu. She was a proud mother of five divine sons, too. Both Karan and Arjun came close to shedding each other's blood but the horror of public shame was so great that it chained Kunti and she watched her sons in a deathly silence. Her eldest son was mocked, taunted and abused by her sons, their teachers, Kripacharya and Dronacharya, but Kunti watched all it with studied silence. Accepting Karan as her son would have weakened her sons' claim to the throne of Hastinapur. Karan's entry in to the family might made Pandavs vulnerable too in palace politics.

Kunti's silence, however, did not stop Karan's progress to glory as he was declared king of Ang pradesh by Duryodhan. It consolidated his enmity with Arjun.

Kunti was registered as a selfish mother in history. She went to Karan a day before the Mahabharat to ask him to spare the lives of her other five sons. She did not declare Karan as her son, she rather pleaded the cause of her 'legitimate' sons with her 'illegitimate' child. She went to him secretly to tell him that she was his mother. She also played on his charitable disposition when he said she had come to ask him for something because he had a reputation of not refusing a request. Karan promised her that at the end of the battle she would still be mother of five sons because at the end of it either he or Arjun would be dead. He promised not to kill any of the other four children.

The most tragic part of this conversation pertained to a mother giving her son his identity but only to save the lives of her publically accepted, legitimate sons. Had she taken him in the family at his first appearance, Karan would not have been by the side of Adharma but on Krishna's side and would have survived.

Interestingly, Kunti did not call the Pandavs to make a full disclosure before them that Karan was their eldest brother. She had Yudhishthir, the Dharmaraj, who would have found a way to bring Karan into the family fold. She also did not ask the Pandavs to spare Karan's life because of the brotherly bond. She asked Karan to do the favour to her legitimate children. Had she come clean before the Pandavs, the picture would have been different, and the war might have been averted.

But she did not explore this alternative of deferring the war because in the heart of her hearts she wished to see Yudhishthir on the throne of Hastinapur. Besides Kunti, Krishna too knew this secret and even he could have told Pandavs, especially Yudhishthir, the truth about Karan. If he had done so, Yudhishthir would not have gone into battle. But any such move would have disturbed the plans of destiny and the script of Mahabharat. Hence, Yudhishthir got to know about this Adharma of killing his own brother by cheating after it had happened.

So the question arises whether the battle of Mahabharat was a larger plot of a premeditated conspiracy and Karan was a mere pawn in this game of thrones? It is the king that has to survive in the game of chess. In Mahabharat, Duryodhan lost all his stakes while the opposite side too could save only five of its pawns.

The battlefield was dominated by the sobs of Kunti. Yudhishthir was astonished to see her mother wailing over the dead body of Karan pierced by Arjun's arrows. A stunned Yudhishthir then asked his mother, "O Mother, why are you crying over the dead body of our enemy, a low born, son of a charioteer?" Kunti's answer sends Yudhishthir into a shock. Despair and remorse descend over the Pandavs who hang their head in shame after knowing that Arjun had killed their own eldest brother.

A shaken Yudhishthir then cursed not only his mother but women in general, too. "Mother, you kept us in the dark about our own blood. Had you told us in time we would not have been the culprits of doing this sinful and unpardonable act. I thus curse the entire woman race that henceforth they won't be able to keep a secret." Ironically, the mother, who moments ago, was an ideal for her sons became a distasteful presence thereafter.

Kunti disappointed in many ways. She failed to open a new vista for women of her time and continued to labor under the feudal system of legitimacy and kingship. She embarrassed her children and her own self by her questionable conduct. Kunti today is not ideal that evokes immediate respect. Instead, became a reason to shame women. Her sister-in-law Gandhari, on the other hand, is placed on a higher pedestal because she took a just stand and also tried to avert the clash between the two royal families. Kunti, in other words, could have done much better but she failed to rise to the occasion every time.

With the progress of the time, the narrative around bad guys of our mythology and history has seen a sea change. Philosophers, writers, analysts have gone deeper into the psyche of the villains to find some good in them. It is said nobody is born a villain, circumstances make him so. Shakuni too was a young prince who transformed into a villain because of his sister Gandhari's unmatched marriage to Dhritrashtar.

Shakuni : The Face of Trickery

In the absence of a villain, there is no hero. In other words, all heroic acts are usually set rolling by the depredations of the counter-hero, the villain. The villain sets the stage for the hero to perform his act. The thicker the darkness, the brighter the light.

Shakuni fitted the frame of a villain perfectly. Shakuni entered Hastinapur with the sole purpose of destroying it as he was incensed over his beloved sister's forced marital alliance with the blind Dhritrashtar. Bhisham Pitamah had initiated the alliance and the King of Gandhar was in no position to object to it in a vigorous manner. Gandhari too agreed to it immediately as she did not want her people to suffer the consequences of war with the powerful kingdom of Hastinapur.

Lord Krishna created Arjun as the hero of Mahabharat by choosing him for the deliverance of divine wisdom through Srimad Bhagwat Gita. It defined righteousness and unrighteousness in great detail. The basic tenet of the Gita focused on the fact Dharma is relevant because of the presence of Adharma. The prevalence of Adharma leads to the rise of Dharma again and again through the manifestation of the Divine in human form. Lord Kirshna was one such incarnation.

On the other hand, Shakuni was nothing but Adharma. His actions not only created a villain like Duryodhan but a hero like Arjun, too. His deception was not an ordinary sport but a calculated move to produce a villain so powerful that the hero needed to adopt unfair means of deceit and trickery to score over him. The Kurukshetra battleground was therefore littered with instances of death by deceit committed by the righteous side – the Pandavs at the instance of the Lord himself.

Lord Krishna detailed the qualities of a soul after it wears a human body. "Every human body does not wear the same qualities. Hence, somebody is hailed a hero and another cursed as a villain," he said. The hero stands tall if he defeats an incarnation of all that is evil.

The beauty of Mahabharat is that it was not a simple moralistic story that ended on a happy note. It rather provided the Pandavs with a tasteless and remorseful victory in the blood-soaked battlefield of Kurukshetra. Only the five brothers and their one wife survived the war while lakhs of soldiers died in the battle. Only one of them was able to step into the paradise and all others were left behind to rot in the hell.

Though Mahabharat has a number of heroes–from Lord Krishna to Bhisham, Dronacharya, Arjun and Ashwatthama --- but there was only one identified villain, Shakuni. He alone bore the burden of creating the heroes of the epic. On a number of occasions, even Duryodhan wavered while committing his villainous acts. But on each occasion, Shakuni led him back to his dark side.

There are a number of reasons that are cited as the root cause of Mahabharat. One of reasons was blind Dhritrashtar's blind ambition to make his son Duryodhan the king after him. The other was Draupadi's hatred for the Kauravs after her disrobing. It is said that notwithstanding these reasons, the war would have been prevented if Lord Krishna had wanted a peaceful resolution to the tussle between the brothers.

But none of these reasons would have come into play without Shakuni. His first pawn in his plan to destroy Hastinapur was none other than his sister's son Duryodhan. He poisoned him against his brothers and ensured that he would not go for a reconciliation with them. With his actions, taunts and jibes, he protested any process of peace and finally succeeded in bringing Kauravs and Pandavs against each other in Kurukshetra.

Mahabharat is actually a grand mix of all sorts of emotions and sentiments. There were also a number of contradictions in its main characters. Bhisham Pitamah pledged himself to celibacy but then took the responsibility of abducting various princesses to become wives of the Kuru princes. He justified kidnapping girls with the purpose of marriage. But then he was not alone in it as Lord Krishna himself exhorted Arjun to elope with his sister Subhadra in order to prevent her marriage to Duryodhan as per the plan of his brother Balram. In one such misadventure, Bhisham fell prey to Amba's curse who ultimately caused his death. Similarly, the marriage of Gandhari to Dhritrashtar prepared the ground for Shakuni's hatred for him and Hastinapur.

Shakuni took an oath to destroy Hastinapur. It was a direct challenge to Bhisham Pitamah's vow to protect Hastinapur at any cost. Bhisham had been granted the boon of choosing the time of his death. He had therefore pledged he wouldn't die till Hastinapur was protected from all sides. Shakuni cleverly caused an implosion in Hastinapur. Bhisham failed to protect the kingdom from its own. Shakuni kept his oath while Bhisham was frustrated in his endeavor.

With the progress of the time, the narrative around bad guys of our mythology and history has seen a sea change. Philosophers, writers, analysts have gone deeper into the psyche of the villains to find some good in them. It is said nobody is born a villain, circumstances make him so. Shakuni too was a young prince who transformed into a villain because of his sister Gandhari's unmatched marriage to Dhritrashtar.

A woman who dearly loved the light had to cover her eyes with a band in order to be one with her husband. The sister's forced sacrifice turned Shakuni into a bitter brother, who proceeded to use his nephew to settle scores with an unjust family of Hastinapur. He sowed the seed of ambition in the mind of Duryodhan and identified the Pandavs as the biggest obstacle on his road to the throne which was actually the road to perdition.

Duryodhan was so influenced by his uncle that he put Pandavs in the category of his arch enemies from his early childhood and tried to kill Bheem by poisoning. The seeds of enmity in Duryodhan developed into a full blown tree by the time he approached his youth. He again tried to kill the Pandavs along with their mother Kunti in the wax palace.

Shakuni in Mahabharat was not an ordinary villain. He was a skilled player of the game of dice which reflected in his conspiratorial behaviour too where he premeditated every move, and had it not been a story Dharma prevailing in the end, he would have done the damage to the Pandavs. It was because of the inevitability of Dharma vs Adharma that Shakuni is not considered to be fully responsible for the battle of Mahabharat. The blame instead fell on the shoulders of Duryodhan, despite the fact that his every action was planned by Shakuni.. His expertise in deception and cheating in the game of dice was the turning point of the epic. Yudhishthir was skillfully tricked by him into a resounding defeat.

No narrative has condemned him for the war. He did have a shot at bravery and his death wasn't glorified. In fact, his death was not described in gruesome detail. He died in silent ignominy. But he was the nucleus around which Mahabharat revolved. Ved Vyas gave his character a number of shades. He therefore plays a number of roles, including that of a villain, a strategist and a comedian. The epic would have been slack without him.

Shakuni knew about Lord Krishna's divinity. But he did not hesitate from playing his role in the events leading up to the war. At one point Shakuni admitted, "Krishna is the only one who may match me in strategic warfare because he is smarter than me."

It became clear as the battle proceeded for nine days that if deceit wasn't matched with deceit, the Pandavs would be defeated and killed. Therefore, Duryodhan's warriors were murdered by cheating, deceit and trickery. The grandsire Bhisham Pitamah, Guru Dronacharya, Karan, Jaidarath and Duryodhan himself were killed by deceit. In other words, had the Pandavs not embraced Adharma to justify Dharma, as guided by Lord Krishna, the result of the war would have been different. The Mahabharat message is simple and clear–end justifies the means.

No piece of literature is complete without the triangle of a hero, heroine and a villain. Mahabharat had a multiple star cast and hence required more than one villain. Shakuni is the lead villain of Mahabharat. He created a number of shadows so as to take down his opponents, including Duryodhan, Karan, Dushshasan, and even Dhritrashtar. It was to his credit that characters like Bhisham,

Dronacharya and Salya were on the side of unrighteousness against righteousness.

The defeat of the villain at the hands of the hero is always the most awaited moment of a story. It is the death of the villain that gives a happy ending. The bad guys have to die or suffer miserably to give the readers pleasure of a justified end. Whether it was Ravana in Treta, Duryodhan, Kansa in Dwapar or Gabbar Singh in Sholay, the villain is always defeated soundly. But the villain survives in the memory of the reader more than the hero. Of late, we have been glorifying crime in our stories and films. Everybody wants to be a Don because crime is something that fascinates and attracts the fantasy of the common man.

As his villainous trait, Shakuni's vow too was no less stern than that of Bhisham Pitamah and he did good or bad effort to fulfill it. He died while making vigorous efforts towards it. Not so Bhisham Pitamah who helplessly watched the fall of Hastinapur before his eyes from the bed of arrows shot at him by his beloved Arjun. Bhisham fought for nine days to secure the boundaries of Hastinapur but on the tenth day he surrendered even as Hastinapur was at its most vulnerable position. Thus, his vow remained unfulfilled like Shakuni's who died without seeing the complete fall of Hastinapur. But Shakuni still had a fair idea that Hastinapur's fall was nothing but a matter of time after his own fall.

Bhisham, on the other hand, instead of accepting his failure to protect Hastinapur appeased his own pride by saying that he might now close his eyes because Hastinapur would be secure under the Pandavs. If that was the case, why did he, in the first place, fought for the Kauravs? Why did he not join the Pandavs and averted the battle? Without him, the Kauravs would not have dared to enter the fight.

Shakuni was the one character who completely justified his role. From day one, he prepared the ground for Mahabharat and ensured that he materialised it. It was Shakuni who created the many heroes of the epic. Had he failed in his design to bring the Kauravs and the Pandavs against each other, there would not have been no Arjun, and even Lord Krishna would not have had a reason to deliver the message of the immortality of the soul.

Shikhandi proved that a woman can destroy a boon and cause the death of Bhisham. Woman were considered a weaker sex and their importance lay in their ability to produce an heir to the family. A woman who burnt herself alive on the pyre of her husband won accolades but she was irrelevant as a widow. She was often discarded by the family and labeled as a witch.

Shikhandi : The Giant Killer

The tenth day at Kurukshetra war was decisive. No doubt that the battle carried on for the next eight days but its result was obvious. A new regime under Yudhishthir was waiting to take over. It was now only a matter of time.

On the tenth day, Bhisham Pitamah was laid low on a bed of arrows by Arjun. The arrows had been shot from behind the person of Shikhandi, a eunuch. Bhisham was blessed with the boon that he could decide the time of his death. Arjun's cowardly act, or his strategic act, of hiding behind Shikhandi wounded Bhisham but he was still alive. Arjun couldn't have killed him despite the subterfuge.

As Bhisham fell, the battle ceased at once to pay respect to the blameless and invincible hero. The Kaurav camp went into a shock and Pandavs, despite their big achievement of incapacitating Bhisham, were joyless and soaked in shame over the way the undefeated warrior had been felled to the ground. There was not a soul on the battleground that was not filled with sorrow and grief, barring Shikhandi, whose vow to kill Bhisham had been fulfilled. Shikhandi, Amba in her previous birth, was composed and satisfied. She had taken birth as an eunuch with a sole aim of causing the death of Bhisham. Her purpose had been achieved.

It was natural for Duryodhan to think that he was invincible because who would be able to kill a warrior with a boon to choose death by own wish. Though Duryodhan had in his side great warriors like Dronacharya, Karan, Jaidarath, Salya and himself, yet it was the presence of Bhisham that was his insurance policy. But the policy had lapsed.

Bhisham was the first strong character we meet on the initial pages of the epic. The son of Shantanu and Ganga was originally named Dev Vrata. To help his father wed his lady love, Dev Vrata took the vow of celibacy. Moved by his son's sacrifice, Shantanu granted him the boon of death by his own wish. Shantanu however did not realise the magnitude of Bhisham's vow or of his boon to the son, and how it would impact his descendants.

Shikhandi proved that a woman can destroy a boon and cause the death of Bhisham. Woman were considered a weaker sex and their importance lay in their ability to produce an heir to the family. A woman who burnt herself alive on the pyre of her husband won accolades but she was irrelevant as a widow. She was often discarded by the family and labeled as a witch.

Bhisham could have been a god without marriage but Amba had no existence or relevance without it. When she was brought to Hastinapur after her abduction, she declared that she was in love with another king. Bhisham asked her to go back to the love of her life, but her lover Salva declined to accept her because he faced a humiliating defeat at the hands of Bhisham when he had tried to prevent him from taking her. Amba returned to Hastinapur deeply embarrassed and insulted. She then asked Bhisham to marry her since he was the one who had abducted her.

The physical or mental health of Kuru princes did not matter to Bhisham. They hardly came in the way for a marital alliance. Kings of other places were keen to cement their alliance with the powerful Hastinapur and offered their daughters in marriage to it. Satyawati left it to Bhisham to forge such alliances. For him, marriage of the Kuru princes became one of his duties. It hardly mattered to him what an abducted princess wanted from her would-be husband. It was because of him that Salva rejected Amba after Bhisham forcibly took her from him. And then Bhisham refused to marry Amba because of his vow of celibacy.

Amba was a strong woman character. He made her choices apparent. He spoke up for herself and her life choices. But the feudal system reacted to her decisions in its own feudalistic way. It used coercion.

Amba was deeply wounded by Bhisham's unilateral methods. Though he was the most powerful chieftain, he relentlessly sought help from other kingdoms to seek vengeance on him. All of them refused to come to her aid. She then undertook harsh austerities to please the gods and seek their help. Lord Kartikeya gave her a garland and said anyone wearing it could kill Bhisham. She offered the protection to several warriors but found no takers. An infuriated Amba, hung the garland at the palace door of King Drupad of Panchal. It is said that she killed herself again and again until she was born to Drupad and was trained in Warcraft. She was a feared warrior until the Pandavs attacked Panchal at the behest of Guru Dronacharya and defeated the Panchal army under her command. After this defeat, she lost favour with her father Drupad. Shikhandi lived every day with a hope of finding an opportunity to kill Bhisham and was happy to join the Pandavs in the great war. Shikhandi knew the much-awaited moment had come.

As the war continued for nine days, the Pandavs became fearful they would lose their entire army. It was at that moment that Lord Krishna gave the advice on how to kill Bhisham Pitamah. Arjun did not like the idea but Krishna told him that it was necessary for the grandsire to fall because he had become the biggest obstacle in the way to establish Dharma. He then called Shikhandi and asked her to ride on Arjun's chariot. Lord Krishna knew that Bhisham Pitamah would not raise his weapon on a woman. Arjun could attack him from using Shikhandi as his cover. The plan was successful. Shikhandi vow was fulfilled.

Shikhandi is also part of a number of political and social narratives. Sage Ved Vyas actually tackled the gender issue through Shikhandi. In her earlier avatar as Amba, Shikhani even puts Draupadi in the shade. She fought for what she thought was her legitimate right. Unlike Draupadi, who nurtured revenge as her second habit, Amba explored it as the last resort. She made every possible effort to save her existence. She had fallen in love and she dared to fight for it. She would have been a happily married princess had Bhisham not disrupted her dreams by kidnapping her from her swayamvar. She then had the courage to admit her love affair in the court of Hastinapur. It was no ordinary feat in view of the then prevailing patriarchal mindset.

A few narratives around Mahabharat say that she was an eunuch while others depicts her as a woman. However, the most accepted theory of her birth was that she was an eunuch but after the battle-lines were drawn, she did rigorous act of penance to convert herself into a woman for a day to cause Bhisham's death. The Pandavs took advantage of her gender change.

However, Shikhandi was the strongest character in Mahabharat and as Lord Krishna said Shikhandi singlehandedly brought the war to a decisive end. It was Shikhandi's tenacity to get justice that stands tall in the epic.

Vidurs, in their modern avatar, make election strategies for the political class. They establish a real-time link between the king and his subjects. However, this class is always very flexible and can easily mix up with any new regime by dumping their previous masters. Vidur was so shrewd that he seamlessly joined the Adharma of Kauravs and later shifted to the Dharma of Pandavs. Vidur, and strategists like him, know it well that their work is to draft strategies. They are however, not responsible for implementing or enforcing them.

Vidur : The Survivor

Vidur was a complicated character of the Mahabharat. Though he was revered by all, the reverence seems manipulated because as the Mahamanrti of Hastinapur he always position himself behind the flag of Dharma. He took advantage of his acceptance as the most intelligent and knowledgeable person of his time to seek a pedestal for himeself.

The author of Mahabharat created Vidur as the flag- bearer of Dharma in the court of Hastinapur even though he registered only a meek resistance to Draupadi's public humiliation in the palace and considered it enough for his role. On the other side, the protest was louder from Duryodhan's brother Vikaran. Yet he was killed in the battlefield, whereas Vidur survived to share the fruits of war alongside the Pandvas after their triumph.

Dynastic rule in the ancient Bharat was never established on merit but on the basis of birth. Since the ruling class was not required to have certain kingly traits to ascend to the throne, it was their birth that made them a natural heir to the crown. The autocracy of the time did everything–from polygamy to black magic–to sire a son. A queen's womb only for the purpose of producing an heir.

The game of thrones though was not that easy to play. The ruling class depended heavily on its strategists --- Vidur in the case of Mahabharat. A clear –headed strategist did half the job for the king through his freight and planning. The ruling class therefore heavily depended on intellectuals who were their ministers, and who would draw up strategy during difficult times. Vidur was the key strategist of the Kuru regime. He was not only a man sought after at the time of war, but also a key adviser in matters of administration and dispensation of justice.

Vidurs, in their modern avatar, make election strategies for the political class. They establish a real-time link between the king and his subjects. However, this class is always very flexible and can easily mix up with any new regime by dumping their previous masters. Vidur was so shrewd that he seamlessly joined the Adharma of Kauravs and later shifted to the Dharma of Pandavs. Vidur, and strategists like him, know it well that their work is to draft strategies. They are however, not responsible for implementing or enforcing them.

Vidur would judge and analyse everybody as his natural right but no one had the right to judge him. Hence, he remained stainless and merged himself with Pandavs after the defeat of Duryodhan with equal ease. Strategists like him are capable of creating their own comfortable climate in every season and survive with all the pelf and power.

When the BJP government decided to re-telecast the Mahabharat, it did not perhaps consider it could become relevant in the time when a pandemic was tormenting the country. The government had put up a brave face and boasted that it would finish off the virus during the time of the first lockdown itself. They had no clue how to face the invisible enemy that was mutating with every blink of the eye. It was under such circumstances, Mahabharat was re-telecast. It brought the greatest of the weathermen Vidur back into focus.

Vidur could read the straws in the wind perfectly. He could also then ensure enough elbow room to keep himself secure from the hostilities of the ensuing bad weather. What is now called a trump card or a masterstroke is Ved Vyas's Vidur neeti.

Every character in Mahabharat was attached to its roots through birth. Vidur was also very important due to his birth. Like Dhritrashtar and Pandu, Vidur was the son of sage Ved Vyas, the creator of Mahabharat. But unlike Dhritrashtar and Pandu, Vidur did not develop in a royal womb and instead came out of a maid. Hence, despite being the most intelligent among his brothers, he was never considered for the throne and carried the ignominy of being called a Daasi Putra (son of a maid). Vidur was acutely aware of his parentage and, as a result, called himself a Daasi Putra at every crucial juncture to keep himself away from the heat.

His frustration was natural because he was not even considered as a successor when Pandu retired to forest along with his wives, and Dhitrashtar was ineligible because of his blindness. The rules were suddenly bent to keep Vidur out and Dhritrashtar was asked to rule in the name of his brother Pandu by Hastinapur's custodian Bhisham Pitamah. It enormously increased Bhisham's importance in the palace.

However, because of his royal parentage, Vidur was given his due and was declared incarnation of Dharma and diplomacy by the author who happened to be his father, too. It is because of Vidur that Dhritrashtar had been earlier dismissed as an heir to the throne due to his blindness and Bhisham had declared Pandu as the rightful heir to the crown. Vidur neeti had then emerged as a villain for Dhritrashtar who accepted his fate and Vidur took the credit for crowning Pandu as King.

Vidur knew he would never be a king because he was born of a maid. He chose the best available option thereafter. He became the king maker. The initial rejection of Dhritrashtar's for the throne prepared the ground for Kurukshetra. Vidur neeti treaded its way thereafter with great caution and extreme vigil to keep its place secure in the court, irrespective of who was the king.

Vidur's astuteness was such that he manufactured arguments to make the same Dhritrashtar king who he had rejected in the first place. Similarly, at the time of the disrobing of Draupadi, he meekly fulfilled his responsibility to protest but remained on the side of the ruling class as a mute spectator of Adharma. He failed to convince Dhritrashtar or Duryodhan against playing the game of dice. It seemed that it was never his intention to stop the game or as a minister he would have owned moral responsibility for the fall of values in the court. Draupadi cursed all present in the court at the time of her cheerharan, including the elders, but Ved Vyas had made Vidur curse-resistant. He thus remained unscathed from the impact of the curse that was otherwise hurled in a general way by Draupadi.

The immunity gave Vidur flexibility to instantly join the winning side after the Pandavs registered their victory.

Despite the Pandavs falling out of favour with the palace and Vidur being a minister of the regime, he continued his relationship with the Pandavs. He did not care about the displeasure of Dhritrashtar and Duryodhan. He knew the importance of proximity to power and he remained with Kauravs. The Pandavs also took him happily as he had never discontinued his connection with them. He had rather helped them by cautioning them from time to time. It was due to his warning that the Pandavs survived the deadly fires at the wax palace.

Vidur never concealed his identity as Daasi Putra. It gave him the leverage of humility and modesty. He never straightaway claimed the throne but kept his lineage to the royalty secure. He was not considered a Kshatriya and hence he was caught between his competence and incompetence in the palace. His frustration exploded on numerous occasions, especially when he kept quiet on contentious issue including the cheerharan or the game of dice.

Vidur is the most relevant character in the post 2014 political scenario that initaited the identity based politics in the country. Like Vidur, top rung politicians declared their caste from the podium of their rallies and played victim. The most secured leader faced the security threat and it was made an electoral issue to garner votes.

Bhisham, on the other hand, was completely free from frustration as far as being a claimant to the throne was concerned. Bhisham never tried to impose his importance on the regime and allowed Dhritrashtar to run the kingdom. Vidur was different. His frustration interfered time and again in the regular run of the administration. All policies and programmes were closely dictated to by Raj Dharma and Vidur monopolised their enforcement. Dhritrashtar was dependent on him when it came to make policies or the rules. The dependence further handicapped him as a ruler. Vidur was perhaps the first most successful politician. His policies are the benchmark for success for any politician even today.

Though Vidur is not a preferred comparison for politicians because his motivation was much more selfish than it is usually seen. He remained with Dhritrashtar until he occupied the throne of Hastinapur but soon joined Yudhishthir after he took over the regime post Mahabharat. The crux of Vidur neeti was to remain with power. The policy makes you certain about your present and keeps you confident about your future. But Chanakya neeti is quoted more often than Vidur neeti because it was not as honest as that of Chanakya.

Like Vibhishan, Vidur too hobnobbed with the enemy of the state he worked for. The only difference was that Vibhishan did it openly whereas Vidur did it in a clandestine way. Vidur knew that Dharma would be on the side of Lord Krishna who was with the Pandavs. His relationship with Dhritrashtar soured on account of Duryodhan as he wanted to keep the alternate option open for himself.

At one stage Dhritrashtar, exiled him from the palace but soon felt alienated and recalled him to court. Dhritrashtar was left with no alternative to Vidur and Vidur too never took any vow not to return to the palace. He returned to Adhrama while keeping his other option of going to the side of Dharma whenever the need arose. His policy was stretchable – it could be pulled to any extent to keep any sort of self- respect at a distance.

This derogation from self-respect is glued to the personality of Vidur because had he allowed pride to come near him he would have to stand against the powers that be. As Gandhari told Lord Krishna that the war could have been averted had he wanted so, the same holds true for Vidur too. On a number of occasion's, he tried to cover the lack of self-respect under the garb of impartiality but he stood exposed as soon as Lord Krishna entered the scene.

Lord Krishna understood the importance of Vidur- type intellectuals in politics. That is why when he comes as an ambassador of peace to Hastinapur to stop the war, he accepts the hospitality of Vidur while rejecting to dine with Duryodhan in the luxury of his palace.

The action prepared the ground of Kauravs' defeat as Lord Krishna successfully cracked the moral confidence of Kauravs even before the first arrow had been shot on the battlefield. Krishna vowed not to take up a weapon, while Vidur never claimed any military skills. But both of them played their role in the war. Krishna was inside the battlefield as Arjun's charioteer. It gave the Pandavs psychological advantage. Vidur broke the morale of Kauravs' from outside the field, before and during the war. Both were thus working for the benefit of Pandavs in equal measure.

Vidur kept himself totally aloof from the war. He rather took a neutral and impartial position right on the onset of the Mahabharat. But as soon as the result was out, he happily joined the Panadavs. One may see the seeds of defection sown by Vidur in politics which have developed fully with the passage of time. Vidur may not be a declared ideal in terms of neeti he practiced but his principles of flexibility and defection are the hallmarks of politics in democracies worldwide.

Vidur is also the initial projection of present-day intellectuals. Vidur represents those people of politics who depend on the mercy of the authority for a place in the power structure. They do not have a mass base of their own. He was like a contemporary minister who loses the Lok Sabha election but is inducted in the Rajya Sabha through the backdoor and then made a minister again. one can count a number of names in this regard.

Duryodhan was a villain but held on to his friends at any cost. Karan is the shining example of his laudable trait. Vidur has no mass support but he was looked upon as one who could create public opinion. It's a simple principle of politics that you can enforce your opinion by sitting by the side of power. Hence, shrewd opinion makers not only enjoy all comforts attached to the ruling dispensation but also jump ships to be with emerging power centres.

Significantly, this section of opinion makers raise their voice in opposition against their own only when they are sure that a shift is in sight. Hence, Vidur neeti was the first visible incarnation of opportunism and defection in corridors of power.

The modern day politics evolved from Yudhishthir's legacy. Its therefore morally corrupt, dishonest, cut-throat, dynastic and selfish. One may learn from Yudhishthir how to interpret and re-interpret a fact or a situation according to one's convenience and the need of the time. Prime Minister Narendra Modi took a dig at former Prime Minister Manmohan Singh for his silence during his two successive governments when he said, "For almost 35 years, Manmohan Singh ji had a lot of influence on country's economic policies. There was not a single corruption charge against him. The art of taking a bath wearing a raincoat can be learnt only from Manmohan Singh." The words of the Prime Minister brought back memories of Yudhishthir and his raincoat.

Yudhishthir : The (A) Dharm Raj

In testing times, objectivity loses its rank as a virtue, and even heroes miss the opportunity to draw a line between the partiality and impartiality. Yudhishthir was one such hero.The Dharm Raj, in fact, failed miserably to take a neutral posture and thus clouded his character in the haze of selfishness and bias.

Though Yudhishthir was the most revered character of Mahabharat after Lord Krishna, he loses his sheen after he failed to live up to the standards of being a satyawadi (truthful) when he accepted a lie in order to ensure the death of his teacher.

None of Yudhishthir's actions bring any clarity to the complex scenario. He instead scrupulously followed the well-trodden path of a feudal set up and patriarchy. In modern times, it is said justice is blind. Yudhishthir's just ways were carried forth with partial blindness. He was unable to see the Adharma committed by the Pandav's side. He threw his weight to establish Dharma by establishing the Kauravs as being unrighteous. He misused the Dharma that he was supposed to enforce to establish his own rule. Despite the grave flaw, he proceeded to heaven because Krishna, Dharma in human form, was on his side.

Yudhishthir was son of the Yamaraj, also known as Dharm Raj. Kunti had invoked Yamaraj to bless her with a son. Yudhishthir came to earth to establish Dharma in a world decaying with Adharma. Yudhishthir faced the most crucial time of his life when his four brothers died by the side of a lake when they ignored the warning of the Yaksh not to drink from it before answering his questions. They took it to be a joke and quenched their thirst. The four Pandavs were said to be obedient to their eldest brother but when they came to the lake to fetch water for him, they preferred to drink it themselves first rather than have it after offering it to Yudhishthir. They also ignored the warning of the Yaksh.

However, when they did not return, Yudhishthir went to look for them and found them dead on the side of the lake. Again, he was so thirsty that he thought of drinking the water first and then take a look at his brothers. The Yaksh, who was delighted that none of the Pandavs could take his questions, warned Yudhishthir not to drink water before answering his questions.

In a majority narratives the four Pandavs failed to answer the questions of Yaksh and fell dead. Some narratives say that they did not even bother to listen to the questions and died as soon as they drank from the lake.

Yudhishthir decided to take the questions and Yaksh, who was his father Yamaraj himself, was happy to put his son to test. But the bigger question is whether there can be one answer to a question? Or there are multiple answers? What about various interpretations of a question and their subsequent answer? Yudhishthir could satisfy the Yaksh with his answers because his answers matched with the answers expected by the Yaksh.

The satisfaction of Yaksh is actually appeasement and is still prevalent in our system. Indian politics is deeply influenced by Mahabharat. And Yudhishthir is its biggest contribution. Yudhishthir teaches us how to change as per the time and circumstances to justify the decisions that are actually desired by you. Yudhishthir did it and yet maintained his honest and truthful reputation. Yudhishthir probably understood the importance of image making and therefore made every possible effort to maintain it at all costs. He committed the greatest Adhrama of killing his own guru, but he continued to be satyawadi by means of a clever device of adding the truth in an inaudible whisper to his loud utterance. It led to the gruesome death of a defenceless Dronacharya.

The modern day politics evolved from Yudhishthir's legacy. Its therefore morally corrupt, dishonest, cut-throat, dynastic and selfish. One may learn from Yudhishthir how to interpret and re-interpret a fact or a situation according to one's convenience and the need of the time. Prime Minister Narendra Modi took a dig at former Prime Minister Manmohan Singh for his silence during his two successive governments when he said, "For almost 35 years, Manmohan Singh ji had a lot of influence on country's economic policies. There was not a single corruption charge against him. The art of taking a bath wearing a raincoat can be learnt only from Manmohan Singh." The words of the Prime Minister brought back memories of Yudhishthir and his raincoat.

If Yudhishthir was the biggest patron of Dharma, his wife Draupadi was the biggest victim of it. He had answered Yaksh with proficiency but was at loss of words when it came to the insults heaped on his hapless queen. Family elders too bathed themselves in the hall of shame wearing the same raincoat. Draupadi was Yudhishthir's biggest test. He failed it miserably.

It did not end here. It was Arjun who had won Draupadi in the swayamvar but when Kunti mistakenly asked the brothers to distribute the 'gift' they had brought for her equally amongst themselves, Yudhishthir failed not only himself but Draupadi too once again. He did nothing to correct the error. Instead, he decided to distribute Arjun's wife to himself and his brothers. Kunti was repentant of her mistake and tried to tell her sons that Draupadi was not a handful of wheat that would be distributed among them. But Dharm Raj had his own interpretation of the situation which was never repeated in any sane society. The end result was that Karan called her a prostitute in the Hastinapur palace.

The vicious insult ironically had been set up by the Dharma Raj himself and when it was hurled he chose to look the other way. He set the wrong example of a husband not standing for his wife and also of treating women as commodity that can be distributed among the men folk without a hitch.

Ironically, it was the time when polygamy had become unacceptable. In the Treta age, Sita was an example of an ideal wife. The elder brother was regarded as a guardian of his younger siblings and their spouses. But Yudhishthir had his own mind. And, because he was the eldest, he became Draupadi's first husband.

Yudhishthir thus dispensed injustice not to one but two women. He made Draupadi undergo the ordeal of having five husbands, while, another woman, Kunti, was blamed for her plight. Yudhishthir touted himself as a son who was merely following his mother's wish. He took no responsibility for the part he played in it and how he did not honor his mother's correction of her mistake. In popular folklore, Kunti is said to be the person who had commanded the sharing of Draupadi among her sons.

Ironically, Yudhishthir was the son who lamented his mother in the middle of the battleground. The war was at its end. A majority of the warriors had been killed. Karan was lying in a pool of blood, dead. To everybody's surprise Kunti was wailing over his dead body. A perplexed Yudhishthir asked his mother why she was crying over their arch rival's corpse. When she revealed that Karan was Pandavs' eldest brother, an incensed Yudhishthir lashed out at her, "Your silence had led to such a macabre war. Lakhs have been slaughtered like animals. Your so called compulsion cost Bharat a lot in terms of blood and death. You are the only person responsible for this dreadful battle. You made us killers of our own eldest brother. O'Mother only if you have not made the wrong choice to be silent. I curse you and the entire female race that henceforth you won't be able to keep a secret." In one stroke, he painted all women with the same brush.

Yudhishthir's third test pertained to his acceptance to gamble in the hall of games. According to the prevailing convention, an invitation to gamble or a challenge to battle could not be declined. Yudhishthir had the opportunity to change this tradition. Instead, he accepted the invitation twice. He agreed to the second one after losing everything, including his brothers and Draupadi to Duryodhan. He lost again and made his brothers and wife undergo the twelve years of exile and another year of incognito life.

Lord Krishna's brother Balram held Yudhishthir responsible for what happened in the hall of games and picked up the gauntlet to stop the practice of offering woman as a stake in various games. "Yudhishthir's Adharma in putting Draupadi as a wager while gambling would make the generations to suffer. So I declare that henceforth no woman would be offered as a stake in any game," Balram issued the order after he saw a woman being offered as a stake in a roadside wrestling match in his own kingdom of Dwarka. On the contrary, Yudhishthir had the dubious distinction of forwarding the decaying system that validated gambling.

Yudhishthir was a reason for the death of his teacher. The Pandavs would not have prevailed till Dronacharya was standing in the battlefield. He agreed to tell a lie audibly followed by a line of inaudible truth. It was a trick. Guru Dronacharya believed Yudhishthir since he was said to always speak the truth. He believed him when he loudly said Ashwatthama had been killed, and whispered–the elephant, not the man. Grief-stricken, Drona thereafter laid down his weapons and was easily killed.

Yudhishthir committed the Adharma of becoming the cause of the death of his guru and a Brahmin, yet he remained unscathed from the adverse impact of the sins because Lord Krishna was on his side.

Yudhishthir, who shattered the trust of his teacher and his wife, preferred to be selfish and look for his own elevation while on his way to heaven. While he approached the road to heaven, his predilection for a dog was more than that for his brothers and his wife. He lost his brothers one after another and also his wife but when reached the doors of heaven, a dog reached there in his wake. Despite objections, he stubbornly asked that the dog should be allowed entry along with him.

Mahabharat leaves its readers with a number of questions, especially after Yudhishthir got into heaven in flesh and blood while his brothers and wife died on the way. Yudhishthir is perhaps the only example of a person entering the heaven without dying. But the question is why only Yudhishthir? Bheem and Arjun had destroyed the forces of Adharma. But since they had done so by deceit, their claim to heaven had been weakened. As an elder brother, Yudhishthir could not guide them away from such acts. He failed his basic duty.

Thanks to him, silence and deception became the biggest strategy of politics. We proudly justify it by saying 'everything is fair in love and war.` But is it so? Recall Draupadi, who was divided between five husbands, and Dronacharya, who died in the grief of his son who was still alive, to realize what Yudhishthir did to his own.

Any character becomes great if he passes the test of time. Lord Krishna shines because of his argumentative partiality and strong and meaningful interpretation of Karma. Yudhishthir was clouded because of his neutrality and the balancing act. He did get his share of respect during the time of Mahabharat but faded faster than expected. He left with no lustre added to his character at the end. He had miserably failed to bring any change during his age and time.

Ironically, the battlefield of Kurukshetra, also called as Dharmkshetra, violated Dharma with impunity. The violations took place not only from the side of the evil forces but from the side of the good one too that was patronised by none other than the God himself. It was in the flicker of the moment that Dhrama mutated into Adharma on a number of occasions in the Dharmakeshtra, including that of the deaths of Karan, Duryodhan, Dronacharya and Jaidrath. Even the grandsire and first commander in chief of the Kauravs army, Bhisham Pitamah, was incapacitated by the indisputable hero of the epic, Arjun, by deceit.

Dharma

Mahabharat is not a mere folklore to be sung in the streets or played on stage. It is a science of human behavior in its true form. Most mythology seems like a work of fiction but Mahabharat is not the same. It does have divine powers and divine entities and they do play their role but the epic never loses its touch of reality and its characters mostly reflect the sinful temptations of love, hate, envy, gluttony, lust, jealousy, rivalry, deceit, cheating and illusion etc. At no point of time, does a reader think that a slice of the real world is not being presented to him.

The epic deals with identifying weaknesses of a person and preparing him to fight them before taking on the enemy outside ourselves. The battle is for improving our Karma that would set our next life in order. The message of Mahabharat becomes loud and clear when Krishna exhorted Arjun to overcome his frailties and to ready his bow to end the evil that was standing before him. When Arjun pointed to his elders and relatives whom he was supposed to fight, Krishna told him that a human body is nothing but a piece of cloth for the immortal soul which it discards from time to time. The message was clear that Kauravs were nothing but representatives of evil so deserved to be destroyed.

"Hence, you must fight without any compunction, as this is what Karma demands. You must do your Karma and not worry about its result. The result is predestined. You are only a medium to perform it. By turning away from your Karma, you would only spoil your next birth, because the soul inside you is immortal. You do not do your Karma on your own peril. And, Hey Parth, what would a warrior do if he would not put up a valiant show of strength against his enemy? It does not behoove of you to show such vulnerabilities at a time when every single person on earth is looking at you to end the evil," Krishna said as he prepared Arjun for the war.

Ironically, the battlefield of Kurukshetra, also called as Dharmkshetra, violated Dharma with impunity. The violations took place not only from the side of the evil forces but from the side of the good one too that was patronised by none other than the God himself. It was in the flicker of the moment that Dhrama mutated into Adharma on a number of occasions in the Dharmkeshtra, including that of the deaths of Karan, Duryodhan, Dronacharya and Jaidarath. Even the grandsire and first commander in chief of the Kauravs army, Bhisham Pitamah, was incapacitated by the indisputable hero of the epic, Arjun, by deceit.

But then this was fair from the slanted angle of the God because it was to protect Dharma and to destroy Adhrama. The Mahabharat was fought to end the feudal system that warranted a king's son to be a king. Duryodhan was fighting for his feudalistic right as his father Dhritrashtar was the King and he considered himself to be the rightful heir to his father. The Panadavs had their own claim.

Ironically, after the Kauravs were crushed, and Hastinapur destroyed, Yudhishthir managed the vast regime on the old feudalistic norms. Thus the entire purpose of Mahabharat was defeated as it justified one feudalistic king with another. Yudhishthir under the command and guidance of God failed to introduce his ancestor Bharat's tradition of a democratic process to choose a king. He rather sat on the throne by exercising his natural right.

Mahabharat however laid the foundation of a penal code that provided punishment to evil. It is still applicable across societies. Any person guilty of any crime is made an example and punished. A war is the last resort after all other law enforcing institutions fail to deliver justice. In Mahabharat, it took years for the Pandavs to face Kauravs in war at Kurukshetra after every other means of reconciliation had failed. Lord Krishna himself approached Kauravs as a messenger of peace but he was not heard. Krishna knew that his effort won't bear result but he still went for peace talks in order to do his Karma. In a human incarnation, even God has to follow the rule of the land.

Lord Krishna delivered to Arjun the significance of Karma. He told Arjun, "Hey Parth, your right lies only over your Karma and not in its result. And you are also not supposed to sit idle thinking that since there was no fruit then why make the effort. Your duty is to do your Karma without any wish for its fruit".

Mahabharat was an epic that was not telling a completely fictional story. It was rather providing direction to future generations to come. Sage Ved Vyas, while writing the epic, was actually penning the do's and dont's for kings, their ministers, army commanders, relatives, art and culture, religion, etiquettes, good and evil.

Lord Krishna successfully carved the concept of a welfare state. It is a principle that is now accepted globally. It underlines the need for a humane state that lives in peace. Though Mahabharat is a celebration in death yet its larger message pertains to a righteous life. It opens new vistas for human beings. The Kshatriya warriors prays to their gods to give them death in the battlefield and they die with a sense of contentment while shedding their blood.

Gita also says that death is the ultimate happening. The body pershies but the soul never dies. Death is not an end but a new beginning. But still everybody tries to dodge death as means the climax of the present life. Gita offers solace to every dying person. It offers salvation from the human form and prepares him for a new beginning.

The relevance of Mahabharat is time tested. Mahabharat's success is in the fact that we still feel connected to it. The government decided to re-telecast during the pandemic when people were locked up in their houses. The government knew that it would surcharge the spiritual and religious emotions in the people.

A classic is evergreen as it can converse with people belonging to different time spans. The characters of Mahabharat are still discussed, redefined and reinterpreted. Questions are asked to its characters and answers are searched on the pages of Mahabharat. Needless to say that a number of such questions remain unanswered because it is not simple to understand Mahabharat.

Today we are looking at Mahabharat with fresh eyes. It is not necessary that Ved Vyas would have written it with the same intentions or aspirations as have been attributed to him. We try to interpret the words in the context of our time and space. Parallels are often drawn and compared to reach a solution. The complexity of Mahabharat or Shrimad Bhagat Gita . however, can be understood from the fact that it is read again and again to find new answers to old questions.

It is said that Mahabharat was actually written by Time. As India developed into a sovereign republic, Mahabharat became its bedrock. The Indian Penal Code is based on the Mahabharat theory of crime and punishment. Mahabharat established that punishment is the most viable solution to tackle crime. Forgiveness has no place in this scheme of things. Lord Krishna minced no words when he said to Arjun, "Your Karma would decide your fate. You should do your Karma selflessly and without any expectation. Leave it to Me, the lord and master of the universe, to decide the result and reward of your Karma."

Paradoxically, Krishna, when he delivered the Gita gyan to Arjun and asked him not to worry about the result, told him that those standing against him deserved death because they were evil and their Karmas were not good. Krishna, in his divine entity, had the ultimate right to punish or reward anybody but he asked Arjun to attack and kill the Kauravs. Krishna, in his human form, had taken the right to punish in his own hands and Arujn became an instrument to punish the evil forces on behalf of God. Even the Kauravs too were pawns who were to be defeated.

The punishment that Krishna gave every one who was evil was death. Death sentence is now strongly opposed and a number of countries have either scrapped the provisions of capital punishment or are contemplating to do away with it.

Mahabharat interestingly starts with a democratic form of King Bharat's governance but ends with the feudalistic rule of Yudhishthir. Bharat ruled ancient India with a conviction and gave utmost importance to one's Karma and dismissed the prevalent notion that succession should be decided on the basis of birth. Hence, he did not make any of his sons his successor and chose his successor from among the people of his regime. He considered himself to be a servant of the people and thought it to be wrong to choose his successor from among his sons. "It would be a betrayal if I chose a successor from among my sons. All my people equally have the right on my throne so I would choose from among them," he said.

And by doing so, Bharat actually created a Dharmkshetra which was converted in a Kurukshetra by Dhritrashtar's love for his son Duryodhan. The foundation of Kurukshetra was though laid by Shantanu by his lust for Satyawati. It was Bharat's blood that took this regressive step and scrapped a magnificent tradition to choose the king from among the public in a democratic way. Karma took a back seat and decision -making fell into the hands of those who took over the reins on the strength of their birth and not their competence.

Circumstances of birth and favouritism became the key to the throne. Dhritrashtar was denied the throne in the first place on account of his physical inability. Dhritrashtar was born blind because at the time of his conception through Niyog (birth without physical contact), his mother closed her eyes because she could not face the stern aura of Ved Vyas. Dhritrashtar's physical inability deprived him of his natural right to succeed the throne.

Vidur, the third son of Ved Vyas, declared Pandu fit for the throne though he later found some dormant royal rule that allowed Dhritrashtar to wear the crown and run Hastinapur under the guidance of Bhisham, an arrangement that could have been made in the first place.

Dhritrashtar lived his entire life frustrated by his blindness. He sought solace in making Duryodhan his successor. The aspiration was considered Adharma and it was decided that Dharma lay in restoring the rule to Pandu's son Yudhishthir. Dhritrashtar's Adharma ultimately led to the war. The great Bharat tradition of finding a successor through democratic norms was lost forever.

After Mahabharat, Yudhishthir became the king, Bheem, the prince, Arjun the protector of borders of Hastinapur, and Nakul and Sahdev became Yudhishthir's body guards. Vidur, who had always been with the Panadavs on the sidelines, was made the main minister. In nutshell, it was nepotism at its best. By confining power to Pandu's sons, Yudhishthir further consolidated the feudal system. In other words, the system of Adharma was restored. Adharma, it seemed, was in the individuals and not in the system though in the times to come the system was judged guilty and discarded in favor of a democratic arrangement.

It is surprising that the God came to earth to establish Dharma but, after many sacrifices, he too favored nepotism. He did not direct the creation of a new balanced system favoring public interest. Pandu's sons' claim to the throne on the basis of their birth was considered to be Dharma while Dhritrashtar move was taken to be Adharma. Krishna replaced the Kauravs with people who were dear to him–sons of his aunt Kunti and uncle Pandu.

It seems that Mahabahrat's wider message is not in the result of the war but in the message of Shrimad Bhagwat Gita that Krishna delivered on the battlefield. Krishna delivered the worldwide acclaimed message of selfless Karma. We do not look at Mahabharat for its consolidation of feudal system but we know it for universal message of identifying and overcoming our weaknesses and to do our own individual effort in the making of a society.

Mahabharat is interpreted by different people in different ways because all of us create our own Kurukshetra and its battle. Sometimes we win and sometimes we lose.

War is no pleasant memory, especially those associated with the land where brothers killed each other to prove their legitimate right of succession to the throne of Hastinapur. India has come a long way from 'Dharmakshetre Kurukshetre' to the land of 'Ahimsa Parmo Dharma.'

Where are you *Krishna!*

"Focus your energies on me. Devote yourself in my supplication. Offer your unconditional devotion to me so as to depend on me completely. And this way you will come to me directly. There is no other place where you may find me."

Lord Krishna said to a wavering Arjun in the moments of his weakness and frustration in fighting his own brothers and elders in the battlefield of Kurukshetra. Arjun was caught in the usual illusions of life and was regressing from the path of his duty that warranted him to do his Karma. An ordinary human being might have rushed out of the battlefield in such depressing circumstances but Arjun was privileged to have the Lord by his side to guide him to protect righteousness. It was the purpose for which both the Kaurav and Pandav warriors had arrayed themselves against each other.

National highway No 1., the gateway to Kurukshetra, the battlefield known to have witnessed the fiercest of battles, awaits Lord Krishna's devotees eagerly every year at the splendor and grandeur of Gita Mahotsav. Successive governments of Haryana have tried to encash on peoples' curiosity about the battlefield and their veneration to Lord Krishna by putting huge billboards of the battle- ready chariot and Arjun blowing the conch to herald the beginning of the war. They have spend thousands of crores on the annual event to attract tourists to this relatively small town that so far has only one feather to its crown. The feather is the battlefield of Mahabharat and the banks of Brahmsarovar where Krishna gave his sermon to Arjun.

People look respectfully at the life-size statues of Krishna which dot the national highway but in a passing way. Not many vehicles that pass this highway venture to take a turn into the city. War is no pleasant memory, especially those associated with the land where brothers killed each other to prove their legitimate right of succession to the throne of Hastinapur. India has come a long way from `Dharmakshetre Kurukshetre` to the land of `Ahimsa Parmo Dharma.`

Ironically, this is the place that made Krishna a globally accepted war hero but his followers prefer to rush to the labyrinthine of Mathura and Vrindavan looking for him to appear before them out of nothing and to have his blessings. Krishna's followers, who run his temples internationally, keep away from the avatar of Krishna as a war-monger. They rather have Krishna by Radha's side as a symbol of undying love and affection.

The magnificence of the Gita Mahotasv, as propagated by the Haryana government, remains on in its audio, visual and print commercials. The fortnight- long celebrations end up like any other run- of- the- mill rural mela where politicians give their speeches and artists present a lacklustre show. Tragically, none of the Haryana governments has ever tried to find out why is it that this glorious event fails to radiate the aura of Lord Krishna.

The utsav therefore comes nowhere close to the appeal of Holi of Braj, the Raas Lila of Vrindavan and Janmashtmi of Mathura. Needless to say that its nowhere near the splendour and solemnity of the Rath Yatra of Gujarat. Krishna's followers from across the globe come to merge themselves in the infinite pleasure of Krishna's presence in the streets and temples of Mathura, Vrindavan and Dwarka but turn their backs to Kurukshetra.

Krishna gave his spiritual message of Gita at Kurukshetra yet even in Haryana Krishna lives more in its folklore than on the battleground. War and death repel people. Hence, the very idea of celebrating Krishna on the battleground is flawed. Though Krishna gave his most important spiritual message in Kurukeshtra yet his legacy lies somewhere else. Krishna is dearly loved as a child, Laddu Gopal, and as a young man who did Raas Lila with Radha. His times as a king of Mathura or Dwarka is hardly remembered with the same affection as his earlier years

Radha is not part of Mahabharat, Rukmini appears alongside Krishna in Mahabharat. But she finds a small mention in the epic. Radha, on the other hand, dominates public mind through the length and breath of the country and is an essential part of the Krishna lore. As a matter of fact, there is no Krishna without Radha.

Mahabharat was written at a time when feudal system was getting strengthened and patriarchy was the law of the land. These two provided the philosophical ground for Mahabharat. It reinforced both of them. It led to a war. No one wants to remember a war. No one wants to hark back to a flawed system that started the war.

In Ramayan, Shambook died at the hands of Lord Ram. In Mahabharat, Eklavya and Karan were the obvious victims of the caste system. The division of class and caste provide philosophic ground for the feudal system. The concept of God and soul cannot get precedence in a feudal society that survives on the vainglory of a system that is built on an uneven foundation. Duryodhan and his coterie refused to accept Krishna, a divine entity, because he was a Yadav though his own father Dhritrashtar, uncle Vidur and grandsire Bhisham Pitamah held him in utmost reverence. Krishna descended on the planet to create a philosophic ground to the concept Dharma and establish the relationship between the soul and the body. But one should never forget that the battleground was only incidental and not consequential as is observed by those who look at the message of Gita with a narrow vision.

Krishna is not merely a human entity in the age of Dwapar. Krishna is the constant flow of time. From his childhood to his youth and up to his death, you meet Krishna in a number of separate avatars. A playful Krishna with a doting Yashoda who raised him as his own child, an innocent Krishna, who lifted a mountain on his index finger or sucked the demoness Pootana to death; a naughty Krishna who stole butter from every household, a smiling Krishna who killed his own uncle after he crossed all limits of tyranny and a young flirtatious Krishna who performed Raas Lila with Radha and her innumerable friends in Vrindavan. Krishna was also friends with Draupadi and came to her rescue during her disrobing. Krishna was friends with the downtrodden too, and preferred Sudama over his rich friends. Krishna refused Duryodhan's palatial delicacies and preferred Vidur's simple food. Krishna, as per the belief system, was omnipresent and omnipotent. He was and is everywhere but it is a matter of debate whether he can be found Kurukshetra.

Krishna in Dwapar is not divine but human. Radha explained to Udhav that the incarnation of Krishna was not divine but was of flesh and blood. A minute study of Mahabharat details the urban and rural divide too. Radha and her friends needed Krishna who lived in a rural Braj household. In Chittorgarh, he was Krishna of Meera who lived in the palace, while in Kurukshetra he was the Krishna of the universe who gave an eternal message of Karma to mankind. Krishna, in fact, is the one that lives in the hearts of the crores of Indians in his naughty boy image and adore the shelves of majority number of households as Laddu Gopal. He is Krishna, he is Keshav, he is Madhav, he is Madhusudan, he is Girdhar, he is Gopal, etc.

Krishna's most loved incarnation lives in Mathura and Vrindavan, where his devotees spend their lives looking for him in umpteen number of temples and in the lanes of Vrindavan. His followers prefer to listen to the soulful music of his flute in Vrindavan instead of the blowing of the bugle of war in Kurukshetra.

Hence, the glamour and pomp of Bollywood dream girl Hema Malini trying her dancing skills to celebrate the spirit of war at the expense of the taxpayers' money in Kurukshetra has invariably failed to attract devotees. People visit the stalls of new agriculture appliances and tractors etc and return home after enjoying pani puri at this mela. At no point of time, they make an effort to find Krishna in Kurukshetra.

For an ordinary citizen, Krishna's message is different than that of the Mahabharat or even the Gita. For them, he is a friend, a teacher, a fighter, a destroyer of the evil, a divine entity to be worshipped, and, above all, a lover. He does not belong to any one person or a sect. He is universal.

Krishna had told Draupadi before the beginning of the war that only her five husbands would survive the impending bloodbath at Kurukshetra. But Draupadi was unflinching in her vengeance. Draupadi did not care for the ensuing catastrophe the war was going to leave behind. Her revenge mattered more than the lives of lakhs of the people. Hence, no one likes to remember Krishna as Draupadi's friend. They instead remember him for his affection towards Sudama and Vidur. In medieval poetry too, Krishna is remembered for his association with Radha, Yashoda, Sudama and Vidur. This is the Krishna that is unequivocally accepted and worshipped as God.